A WOMAN and HER

Emotions

What Every Woman
Needs to Know

Gayle Roper

BEACON HILL PRESS
OF KANSAS CITY

Copyright 2007
By Gayle Roper

ISBN-10: 0-8341-2325-8
ISBN-13: 978-0-8341-2325-0

Printed in the
United States of America

Cover Design: Darlene Filley
Interior Design: Sharon Page

A Woman and Her Emotions is the revised and updated text of *Balancing Your Emotions* published by Harold Shaw Publishers in 1992.

10 9 8 7 6 5 4 3 2 1

For Ashley, as she takes that first great step into adulthood.

Congratulations on your graduation, and may your heart always be so committed to the Lord.

Contents

Introduction

When I was a kid, I went to church with the people who lived down the street. My parents, wonderful people, were concerned for me when, as a young teen, I committed my life to the Lord. They were afraid I would become a fanatic. One of their tactics to show me the fallacy of my ways was to point out the problems of many of those who went to my church.

Mom and Dad were never malicious, and they thought they were doing me a favor. I have never doubted that. However, the failures of the believers were salt crystals rubbed against my wounded heart. Why couldn't people who claimed Christ just live the way He wanted them to?

There are many possible simplistic answers to this very complex issue, but one reason is lack of emotional constancy. This truth was brought home to me as I took classes in pastoral counseling and talked with clients whose lives were in chaos because of either their own lack of emotional restraint or that of others who had deeply hurt them.

Emotional constancy, emotional consistency, emotional balance. Call it what you will. It's what this book is all about.

I want to thank my writer friends who shared their insights with me for this book: Carolyne Aarsen, Charlene Baumbach, Shelly Beach, Mindy Starns Clark, Athol Dickson, Rene Gutteridge, Angela Hunt, Ethel Herr, Jane Kirkpatrick, Harry Kraus, Dandi Daley Mackall, Gail Gaymer Martin, Nancy Moser, and Camy Tang.

Identifying Emotional Chaos

We experience emotional chaos for a variety of reasons—reasons that are not always clear to us in the midst of daily dilemmas. The first step toward consistency under stress is to identify the causes of our emotional ups and downs.

In the first seven chapters we'll talk about health and its potential effects on our emotions. We'll discuss the influence of self-esteem as well as our dreams and goals on all we are and do. We'll analyze the confusion when our feelings lead us around by the nose or when we have no patterns on which to build a balanced life. And we'll discover the difference between *real* guilt and *assumed* guilt so that we can break free of the emotional ropes that bind us.

1 Are Emotions Ever Trivial?

> Junior high school and emotional chaos go together like
> spring and baseball. Thankfully, we age.
> —Gayle Roper

Remember junior high school? Ah, yes, I saw that shudder. For most of us, those years are a time we'd just as soon forget.

I remember one specific day in eighth grade. I stayed after school for some long-forgotten reason. When it came time to go home, all the friends I usually walked with had left. I had to walk a mile and a quarter *alone.*

What if someone *important* saw me walking alone?

What if someone *unimportant* saw me walking alone?

What if the people who lived in the houses I had to pass saw me walking alone?

My stomach churned with tension, and my eyes blurred with tears of embarrassment. The world was about to discover my ghastly secret, one I tried to deny even to myself: I was unpopular.

Staring miserably at the sidewalk, I began my journey. I didn't dare look up because I might see the curtains twitching as I passed the houses. If I didn't see the faces staring out the windows, then I wouldn't hear the whispers, "That poor girl. She's walking by herself. Obviously no one likes her."

I had gone a block and a half when out of the corner of my eye I saw movement on the other side of the street. Cautiously I looked over.

It was Sylvia!

A situation I had thought the ultimate in self-conscious agony suddenly escalated right off the mortification charts. Sylvia was an upperclassman, and to my young eyes, she was all that I wasn't: beautiful with glorious red hair, popular, a cheerleader. She even had a figure, something I was still sadly lacking. Worst of all, she lived on my street. That meant she would see me walking all alone the whole way home. I had never known such humiliation and shame.

It wasn't until years later that it finally dawned on me that Sylvia was alone too—and who cared?

From my present vantage point as a Titus 2 "older woman," it's hard to admit that I was foolish enough to feel such emotional pain over such a trivial situation, but I did. It seemed perfectly logical to me that people had nothing better to do than look out their windows and comment on a girl walking home by herself. It also seemed utterly reasonable that Sylvia's thoughts should focus on me and my shame.

Now I can only shake my head in amazement and thank the Lord that I will never be 13 again. I imagine that most of us do not want to face the emotional chaos of hormones kicking in, self-esteem taking a hike, and popularity becoming the Holy Grail ever again. A return to that time would be the equivalent of experiencing anew the worst toothache we ever had or going through the agony of natural childbirth again, only this time the pain lasts for three or so years.

But even now there are times when my emotions rise up and surprise me. I'm not speaking about times when I could expect to feel emotional—weddings, funerals, graduations, births. I'm speaking of the unexpected, unforeseen explosions of emotion that can turn a day upside down.

A few years ago I was taking graduate work in counseling. Halfway through one semester I was placed under the oversight of a new professor. He observed me with two clients I had been seeing for several weeks. It was the responsibility of the new professor to meet with me after the sessions and critique my work, just as the former instructor had done.

This new teacher found fault with my work like no one ever has before or since. He very kindly tore to shreds everything I had done. I remember no positive comments whatsoever.

I responded to his comments in my usual way when things get too emotional—I said nothing because I knew if I opened my mouth, I'd cry. I was afraid that tears might destroy whatever remained of my academic hopes.

I left his office and drove home, talking to myself the whole time. "You go to graduate school, kid. You're playing in the big leagues. If you can't take the heat, the kitchen door is in the rear."

In spite of my mixed metaphors, I managed to get myself under control. When I got home, I told my husband, Chuck, about my victimization.

"He never took into consideration that I'd already established a relationship with these folks. He tore into me unfairly."

I basked in Chuck's sympathy and managed not to cry. I went to bed and prayed myself to sleep, allowing a few tears in the Lord's presence. After all, He's been there and heard the whole thing.

Something woke me in the middle of the night, and I got up to check on the kids and the cats. Not wanting to waken

Chuck, I didn't turn on the light. As a result, I walked full tilt into our partially opened bedroom door, cracking my head just over my right eye.

Then I cried. And cried. Poor Chuck wakened from a deep sleep to find me wailing my heart out in the dark in the doorway.

My emotions had crept up and grabbed me when I wasn't expecting them. Certainly I hurt my head, but not enough to merit my dramatic reaction. It was retroactive pain I was memorializing.

Without a doubt, our emotions are a gift from God to give our lives richness and meaning. We laugh and cry and love and hurt and yearn. Little arms loop around our necks, and we go squooshy inside. Someone makes a particularly nasty remark, and we simmer or withdraw. A friend suffers a major or minor loss, and we grieve with her. Another friend gets a much-deserved promotion, and we rejoice. All these feelings can deepen us, enrich us, and make us more thankful to God and/or more dependent on Him.

Or they can confuse us, warp us, and make us forever 13.

Recently a young woman told me that she didn't think women today struggled with their emotions. Her implication was that we are now so sophisticated that we always have everything under control. We never struggle with negative feelings and always embrace positive, God-honoring attitudes.

I blinked, trying to imagine the women she knew. They certainly were different from me and my friends. Did they never get lonely or hurt? Did they no longer yearn for meaning, for fulfillment, for love? No longer struggle with how to handle a cutting remark or search for the best way to overcome an unforgiving heart or fight their feelings of defeat and failure in an unhappy life situation?

I'm convinced that we all struggle at times over things both little and big. We get out of bed on the wrong side and spend the day fighting our nasty, sarcastic, critical, or accusatory alter egos. The family is grumpy at breakfast, and before we know it, their negativity has us yelling or complaining or walking off in a huff. Novelist Gail Gaymer Martin notes that even the weather can play a strong role in our emotions. "A week of gloomy skies and rainy days can affect a woman's decisions and attitudes more than the issue she's struggling with itself."

Perhaps we're among the many who live with big issues and constant stress, and the tension makes us emotionally vulnerable to melancholy or resentment or bitterness. These negative emotions subtly seep into our conversation, our relationships, and our hearts, often without our even noticing. Novelist Nancy Moser tells of a spring when she was extremely stressed.

My youngest was graduating, I had heavy deadlines, there were normal family crises and upheavals. I had a list of 34 things to do—*now*. During all this I was writing a manuscript and managed to turn it in on time on June 1. When I received the editor's initial review of the book, she commented on the anger and bitterness of the wife-character, the total unlikability of the husband-character, and the general in-your-face negativity of the book. I was shocked that the emotions I was experiencing were so blatantly revealed in the work. It was a wake-up call to me as a writer. I had to completely rewrite the book.

Most of us aren't writing novels, but our pessimism or anger or hopelessness will find a way to color our worlds too. Sharp tongues, critical attitudes, and spite seep out, painting everything we touch in shades of peeve green, foul-tempered black, or I-give-up gray. We say and do things that cannot be unsaid or undone.

So what can we do when we want emotional peace but all we create or experience is inner chaos?

The purpose of this book is to look at seven things that give many of us women problems emotionally and then examine them in the light of Scripture. We'll study the effects of poor health, the inevitable disappointment of wrong goals and expectations, the anxiety of an improper view of self, the turmoil caused by emotional anarchy, the damage from a lack of life patterns, the burden of assumed guilt, and the weight of real guilt. Then we'll study six things that may well give us a handle on living in that peace that passes understanding. We'll talk about the freedom of confession, the release in the old self/new self principle, the efficacy of practice, the challenge of contentment, and the blessing of daily commitment.

Our goal, of course, is to find emotional balance, giving

ourselves the ability to enjoy the good things in our lives and the means to control the negative feelings.

Novelist Jane Kirkpatrick writes of the burden basket used by many of the native peoples of the West. "These were largely nomadic people and only put essentials in their burden basket as they had to carry everything with them. A tumpline of leather around their foreheads kept the baskets, shaped like whirlwinds, in the center of their backs. But it was also important that the contents of the basket be balanced so unnatural pressure wasn't placed on one side of the neck and head."

Jane continues, "It's been my experience that women often put more than the essentials in the things they carry around with them. Old hurts, disappointments, anxiety, guilt, all get carried, leaving little room for the real essentials like love of God, family, and friends. In addition, they stuff their worries into the bottom of the basket where they are hard to reach and consequently hard to deal with."

If you find yourself feeling defeated, guilty, inordinately worried, anxious, or inadequate, there is help. By the grace of God, emotional constancy can become yours.

What Do You Think?

1. What are the main benefits of living with an emotionally consistent individual? _____

_____

_____

2. Are you such an individual? What are your emotional strengths? What are your emotional weaknesses? _____

_____

_____

_____

3. Can you think of anyone in your life who has modeled emotional constancy for you? What was the greatest benefit of knowing that person? _____

_____

_____

_____

4. How about someone who was emotionally inconsistent? What influence did this individual have on you? _____

_____

_____

_____

5. Read Col. 3:12-17. What does this passage say to you about emotional consistency? Which of these positive qualities is hardest for you to practice? Why? _____

_____

_____

_____

How Do You Feel?

2 The Health Factor

My, that *is* a typo. So you were expecting the collagen
injection in your *lips* and the liposuction in your *hips*.
—Dave Coverly, *Speed Bump*

I first found out about the profound impact of health on
our emotions through my husband. For several years
Chuck struggled with low-grade anxiety that would unexpectedly explode into fear.

The problem developed when he was in graduate school, and at that time he sought help from a Christian counselor. The gentleman was very kind and sympathetic, but he had no particular advice and no practical help except to recommend that Chuck take a job at a smaller company when he finished school. His theory was that Chuck's work stress would be less.

Chuck followed this advice, but the anxiety still persisted.

I was distressed by the changes this condition made in my husband. When I first met him, he was almost too cocky, too sure of himself. He loved to lead or speak in public. He was tall and slim and very handsome, and he excelled at athletics. He'd always done well academically and was in a doctoral program when we married. I felt I'd never have to apologize for him or be embarrassed by him. Like my father told me the first time Chuck came to dinner, "He's the best thing you've brought home yet."

When this anxiety condition developed, all that self-assurance disappeared. Now it was torture for him to do something as simple as read a Bible verse in a small-group setting. To get up in front of a larger group was beyond him.

When Chuck settled in his job, the pressures of graduate school gone, the anxiety abated somewhat, but it never went away. For 12 years he struggled, constantly seeking the Lord's help. For 12 years the situation remained the same.

"It must be a spiritual problem," he'd say periodically. "After all, the Bible says to not be anxious about anything, and

I can't seem to manage that no matter how hard I try or how much I pray."

But neither he nor I could see anything in his life that would indicate a spiritual deficiency. Chuck was faithful in his walk with the Lord. He served in our church. He was an excellent and caring husband and father. His speech was always flavored with grace, and he was as consistent and kind in our home as he was in public.

I knew I couldn't see into his secret heart, but actions inevitably flow out of the heart and mind. There simply was nothing to indicate a continuing sin problem. In fact, all evidence pointed to just the opposite: my husband was a godly man.

Finally Chuck said, "I have to get help for this. We've struggled long enough." And off he went to another counselor.

One of the first things this counselor did was send Chuck for a full physical, including a blood workup. And, presto, chango! We found the culprit: hypoglycemia.

The characteristic hallmark of hypoglycemia is low blood sugar, a measurable abnormality. Sugar, or glucose, provides energy to the body and clarity to the brain, and when the glucose level in the body isn't high enough, trouble occurs. In hypoglycemia, the pancreas produces too much insulin, which in turn suppresses the body's glucose, in contrast to diabetes where the pancreas doesn't produce enough insulin to regulate the body's glucose.

The brain is particularly sensitive to insufficient glucose, and when it's deprived, impaired function occurs. Mental wooziness, anxiety, and sleeplessness are some of the results.

Chuck was advised to follow a high-protein, low-carbohydrate diet eaten in several small meals a day. Like a diabetic, he was told to eat no sugar. For a guy who could eat a package of cookies in a single sitting and daily buried his cereal in the granulated white stuff, the sugar-free diet was torture, especially at first. But almost immediately he felt so much better that he persevered even until this day, many years later.

The point of this story is that what Chuck was suffering from was not in any way spiritual. It was physical. His low blood sugar was playing terrible games with his brain and therefore his emotions.

Novelist Rene Gutteridge says:

> I'm just starting to realize how much diet and medicine play into our emotional state as women. The thing about emotional imbalance is that it feels normal after a while. And no one talks about it. We pull ourselves together and pretend everything's okay while we're in public when we should be acknowledging how we feel and seeing a doctor or therapist or counselor or friend. When I started eating healthfully, my emotions straightened out. I began sleeping better, and I didn't have to deal with the fatigue I had battled every day.

It's important to consider the relationship of health and emotional consistency for two reasons:

1. If health is somehow negatively affecting our emotions,

a treatment may be as close as a good doctor and a healthful diet.

2. Pinpointing the problem as physical may help us avoid the it-must-be-spiritual-therefore-I'm-a-lousy-Christian trap.

❈ ❈ ❈

Menstruation

Because of our gender we women live the majority of our lives with the effects of bodily functions on our emotions. From the time we begin menstruation at approximately 12 years of age until we complete menopause at 55 or so, our monthly cycle affects our disposition and our behavior.

I have very clear memories of suffering terrible menstrual cramps each month as a teenager and young woman. I remember the day in high school I stood waiting by the door for my mother to come take me home because I felt so terrible.

One of the guys in my class walked by. "Wow, Gayle," he said. "You look green."

I felt green, and we all know, thanks to Kermit, that it's not easy being green.

I lived at home my first year out of college. I taught junior high school, and my father, also a junior high teacher, gave me some excellent advice.

"Keep control of your class, Gayle," he said. "Don't try to be the kids' friend. In fact, don't smile until after Thanksgiving. Take care of your own discipline problems; don't send them to the office. And whatever you do, don't be one of those women who takes off a day every month."

Uh-oh, I thought when I heard that last line. *I'd better always start my period on Saturday.*

Besides the physical pain that may be involved monthly, menstruation can also include emotional pain brought on by physical conditions. Premenstrual syndrome (PMS) is an all-too-common problem for many women. Exactly what causes it is not known, though there is much research being done about hormones causing neurochemical changes in the brain or the retention of fluid putting pressure on the brain. There is no specific diagnostic test for PMS. The cyclical nature of the symptoms is the best indicator.

The physical symptoms of bloating and discomfort are a trial to any woman who struggles with PMS, but it's the emotional ugliness—anger, irritability, and depression—that makes women cringe when they hear themselves or see the faces of family and friends who have become the targets of their latest outbursts. For a Christian woman, this disturbing instability evokes guilt and feelings of letting God down.

It's all too easy to yell, "PMS made me do it!" But PMS isn't license to lose all control. We are always to be kind and considerate, always to speak with grace. We are to apologize when we fall short. However, we must also give ourselves some latitude, especially if we are among the 5 to 10 percent of women who suffer severely. At the same time, we have to act responsibly and seek help. There's much that can be done medically to level out the symptoms of PMS. There are also easy-to-do steps like limiting salt and caffeine, eating six small meals a day, exercising, and taking vitamins that can help.

For more information go to www.womenshealth channel.com or www.4woman.gov. Both offer excellent information on PMS and many other health issues for women.

❊ ❊ ❊

Postpartum

Another time when physical changes play heavily on emotions is postpartum. Two or three days after delivery over 80 percent of new mothers feel weepy and lost because of the rapid changes in estrogen and progesterone levels in their bodies. These "baby blues" may last up to a week but pass spontaneously and are nothing more than inconvenient.

However, for 1 woman in every 10, postpartum depression (PPD) sets in, lasting three to four months post-delivery. And 1 in 1,000 may experience postpartum psychosis (PPP), a condition so severe that a mother may wish to take her baby's life. Again, hormones are the culprit, and the conditions are treatable. "Please remember that with good medical or psychiatric intervention, these illnesses are treatable and the prognosis is excellent," reads the statement at the bottom of the home page at www.depressionafterdelivery.com.

Depression After Delivery, Inc. is a national support organization for women who struggle with PPD or PPP and related issues. This organization's Web information is excellent, and for those not Web literate, the number is 1-800-994-4773.

❊ ❊ ❊

Menopause

Another emotionally volatile time for us women is menopause. Hot flashes, palpitations, mood swings, difficulty concentrating, changes in hair and skin, and changes in sexual function mark what is called the climacteric, the whole physiological process of losing our fertility. This season of life lasts from 6 to 13 years.

Once again, a good doctor is essential to help plot a course that will diminish the most irritating or debilitating symptoms. Anyone who has wakened in the night drenched from a hot flash or night sweat, her sleep once again interrupted by all that heat trapped beneath the covers, yearns for something to diminish the sheer frustration of the situation. A good night's sleep looks as unattainable as it did during the days when her babies didn't sleep the night through.

In spite of the recent doubts about Premarin, and especially about the combination of Premarin and progestin, there are courses of treatment that are safe. Some are herbal; some are prescription. Some are right for you. For more information, try these Web sites: www.menopause.org, the site of the North American Menopause Society, which has an academic feel; www.americanmenopause.org, the site of the American Menopause Foundation, which is also academic in feel; www.power-surge.com, a chatty and warm site dedicated to menopause; and www.primeplususa.com, home of Prime Plus/Red Hot Mamas, also personal and inviting.

Not that long ago, reaching menopause was the sign that a

woman was old and her life was almost over. Not so anymore. Today, we live almost a third of our lives postmenopause. We mustn't look at this time as the beginning of the end. Rather, it's the beginning of the beginning. Opportunity beckons. Maybe it's time to finally go to college or to go back and finish that degree; it's never too late. My mother began her undergraduate work when she was 48 years old and graduated with honors at 55. I began a master's program at 54. Maybe you can start that business you've always wanted or open that tea shop or craft store. Take those ballet lessons. Go swimming every day and get involved in the senior Olympics. Organize that neighborhood Bible study. Bake wedding cakes for all your friends' kids' weddings. Write a book.

❊ ❊ ❊

Depression

We call it clinical depression; the ancient Greeks called it melancholia and noted how debilitating it was. This type of depression, different from PPD, can be rooted in emotional issues, but often it's physically caused. Faulty neurochemistry leads to faulty thought patterns, skewed emotions, deep sadness, and may include excessive fears or obsessions. Life becomes black and hopeless, the future frightening.

If depression strikes you or someone you love, chances are that the cure is not as simple as thinking happy thoughts or trusting in the Lord, no more than these activities are cures for a broken leg. Certainly God can heal someone of depression, and sometimes He does. Usually though, He asks the victims to learn to live with the illness, much as He asks one suffering from rheumatoid arthritis or diabetes to.

All over the world today, women experience this deep, debilitating depression more than men. In the United States, where 19 million suffer some form of the disease, women are afflicted twice as often as men. "Most depression can be treated effectively. . . . Given its enormous effect on the quality of life, no woman should hesitate to ask for help from her primary care doctor or a psychologist or psychiatrist, pastoral counselor, or other qualified mental health professional."[1]

❀ ❀ ❀

But Isn't Sin, Sin?

In considering the emotional effects of physical conditions on women, we come to an interesting and critical crossroads of thought.

What does the Bible have to say about the tie between our emotions and actions? Even if we "can't help it," doesn't it hold us personally accountable for all our wrongdoings? Isn't sin, sin whatever its origins? Isn't anger always wrong when it attacks and hurts? Isn't speaking to get even or losing one's temper always displeasing to God?

"Even though we are always accountable before God and responsible for sinful behavior, the Bible adds important qualifiers," writes Dr. Ed Welch. "Scripture qualifies that though we are always morally responsible, we are responsible according to the responses of our hearts. . . . We are also responsible according to our gifts, talents, abilities, knowledge, and understanding. . . . This puts Christians in the unique position of upholding universal biblical standards while simultaneously being sympathetic to individual differences in abilities."[2]

Consider Molly, a woman with severe PMS who has recently become a Christian. Molly suffers from an attention deficiency and, though she is very intelligent, she barely graduated from high school because of her disability. She has a pattern of screaming and yelling, even on good days, but especially at PMS time. When she becomes a shrew, she says she can't help it. It's PMS.

Caryn suffers from PMS also, but she's been a believer since childhood. She has set her heart on living for God, and she deeply loves Him. She enjoys studying the Bible and is an accomplished Bible study teacher. When she gets all nervy and mouthy as a result of PMS, she can't decide whether she is justified in excusing herself (after all, it's of physical origin) or guilty of sinning.

When Dr. Welch speaks of responses of the heart and differing abilities, he is speaking of things like Molly's spiritual infancy and Caryn's longtime relationship with God as well as Molly's learning disability as contrasted to Caryn's enthusiastic studying.

Caryn can rightfully be expected to control her PMS instead of yielding to it, to make an effort to live in a godly pattern even when it's exceedingly difficult. She can also be expected to understand God's grace and forgiveness when she fails and to seek medical assistance more quickly.

Molly will learn very slowly about personal responsibility and the fact that she should not throw her hands helplessly in the air and say whatever she wants. It will be harder for her to grasp that there is medical treatment available and to follow through on its use. In the meantime, she will continue to be a wild woman on certain days, and God will continue to love her and forgive her and teach her the way He wants her to behave.

> Brain dysfunction, at least if the affected persons are alert and responsive, does not affect the moral capacity of the heart. Therefore, those with brain impairments must be treated as image bearers like everyone else. To treat them differently would be disrespectful, prejudicial, and unbiblical.[3]

So sin is sin, we are responsible for our actions, but we understand that everyone isn't able to perform at the same level. While the goal is always to live in a way that honors Christ, even on PMS days, the gift of God is forgiveness when we fail.

❋ ❋ ❋

I have always thought it a special blessing to be a woman. Our minds can be as keen as men's, but we usually have a sensitivity that men don't. Whether this sensitivity is cultural and learned or innate is not the issue with me, though I come down on the innate side. Wherever it comes from, we have this heart-consciousness. Isn't it a tragedy of the highest sort if a treatable health problem limits the use of this great capacity to love, to encourage, to sympathize, and to model the heart of God?

❋ ❋ ❋

Summary

Health problems can have a great impact on us emotionally.

Just being a woman forces us to deal with physical issues for the majority of our lives.

PMS, postpartum difficulties, and menopause put special stress on our emotions.

While physical changes in our bodies affect our brains and may make emotional consistency difficult, we are always responsible to the level of our knowledge and abilities to live in godly patterns.

❋ ❋ ❋

What Do You Think?

1. Have you had or do you presently have a physical problem that has affected your emotions? What has helped you cope?_____

_____

_____

_____

2. Read John 9:1-3; 2 Cor. 1:3-4; and 2 Cor. 12:10. What are some of the reasons God allows sickness and weakness?

_____

_____

_____

3. Elizabeth Cady Stanton, an early suffragette who lived actively into her 80s, wrote in her autobiography that "the heyday of a woman's life is the shady side of fifty."[4] What do you think Mrs. Stanton meant and do you agree? _____

_____

_____

_____

4. When your emotions do get the better of you at that time of the month or that time of your life, what should you do about it? First John 1:9 is a good place to start. _____

_____

_____

_____

_____

5. Does your doctor understand the special problems of women? How do you know? What should you do if he or she does not? _____

_____

_____

_____

How Do You Feel?

3 Dreams and Disappointments

> Goals are just dreams with deadlines.
> —Lenora Worth

I've been a writer for more than 35 years, and I assume I have the same dreams and goals as other writers.

I dream that people will read my work on purpose rather than by default.

I dream that people will walk into bookstores by the droves and say to the clerk, "Do you have Gayle Roper's latest book? I've been waiting for it, and it's finally out!"

I dream the clerk will say something besides, "Who?"

I dream that the bookstore will actually have a display of my books in one of those cardboard endcaps, the things that everyone trips over at the end of the aisles. I dream that such a display might even be right inside the front door where customers can't miss it.

I dream that editors will fight to publish my books, that my work will be the object of a bidding war between publishers.

I dream that at the big Christian retailing show for bookstore owners I will have an autograph booth all my own with a line of people that stretches out of sight, all of them seeking my autograph.

I dream that I will actually make some money with my writing.

But I'm not holding my breath.

Everyone has goals and dreams, those unspoken yearnings of the heart that we never voice because they are too private, too precious, too impossible by commonsense standards.

Ginny was full of goodwill and the warm flush of obeying the Lord's call to service when she volunteered to teach Sunday School. "I want to tell these first graders about the grace and glory of the Lord while they're little so that their young lives will be steeped in Scripture. Then they might not make bad choices later in life. When they're little like this, they listen. They accept truth when you teach it to them."

Ginny dreamed that the kids would say, "Thank you, Miss Ginny. You're the best teacher I ever had. You taught me how to love Jesus."

Then she went to class and actually tried to teach.

When she got married, Joy was full of bright hopes and big expectations; everyone's good wishes were ringing in her ears. She set her goals high: she wanted a wonderful Christian marriage, the kind people would look at and sigh over, the kind that would be a good testimony for Jesus to all who knew her.

"I love Lou so much, and he loves me. I know I'll always be there for him, and he'll always be there for me. We will not make the mistakes I've seen in other marriages. People will be able to look at us and think, *That's what a marriage should be.*"

Then she started living with the flawed man she married.

Arlene looked at the tiny, dependent bundle suckling at her breast. She couldn't believe how perfect he was, how absolutely wonderful. Her heart was full of wishes and prayers for this little one: happiness, security, love, success, a strong and personal relationship with Christ. "We won't have the difficulties I had with my mom, the tensions and fights and demands. With the help of the Lord we'll avoid them. My son will always know I love him and am there for him."

As she smoothed her hand over the baby fuzz on his little head, she could hear him saying, "I love you, Mom. You're the best!"

Then the child turned 2, then 12, and then 18.

Ginny, Joy, Arlene, and I have set ourselves up for potential failure when we set our goals, for two reasons:

- Our expectations are unreasonable.
- They cannot be fulfilled without the appropriate actions of others.

Problem No. 1: Unrealistic Goals

There is nothing wrong with having high goals. It's wise to hope and plan and try. If we don't attempt, we'll never achieve. We need to pursue these goals with determination. As novelist Charlene Baumbach says, "I relentlessly pursue all things that are important to me, including God, family, friends, ministry, and rest. In other words, I don't give up on what matters to me."

Charlene's attitude is good, and she's absolutely right—we should pursue our dreams wholeheartedly. However, tempering our dreams with a little reality isn't bad either. It can remind us of how fantastically high our goals may be and how few people actually breathe the air at that level of achievement.

Take my writing goals. Basically I'd like all my books to be best sellers and my name to be recognized by thousands of readers. However, when you think about it, not many writers out of the hundreds of thousands practicing the craft actually make the best seller lists. How many writers' names can you rattle off as ones you seek out? How many times do you buy a book because of who the author is as opposed to the topic or catchy cover and blurb?

Quite simply, the numbers are against me.

Ginny may make a difference in the lives of her Sunday School charges, but her idealism may be causing her to forget that six-year-olds have an incredibly short attention span and enough undisciplined energy to light New York City.

Joy, who wants the perfect marriage, wants a fine thing. She's just forgetting that two sinners who marry cannot produce a perfect marriage no matter how much they want to or how hard they try.

Arlene wants a wonderful parent-child relationship, a most worthy dream. But to expect no tensions between her and her son—especially when he begins seeking independence as a teenager—is to open herself to great disappointment.

Problem No. 2: Dependent Goals

For me to achieve my goals as a writer, I am dependent on an incredible number of people:

- an editor who likes my work and helps me develop it
- a publishing company that is willing to publish it
- an artist who designs an eye-catching cover

- a marketing department that pushes the book
- salesmen who talk it up to store owners
- store owners who stock it—and restock it
- several thousand readers who buy it

The odds of all these things falling into place with the necessary numbers are incredibly slim. I know the Lord can work miracles on my behalf, but the truth is that there are many thousands more writers whose names go unrecognized than famous ones. To put all my eggs in the basket of best-sellerdom is to ask for disappointment.

Ginny, who wants to be a wonderful Sunday School teacher, is dependent on her students for success. And we all know that students don't always cooperate.

Joy must depend on her husband for her perfect marriage scenario, and nice as he may be and try as he might, he can't be or do all she wants.

Arlene must depend on her child for that perfect mother/son relationship, and anyone who's ever been in a family knows that differences of opinion, taste, age, and standards cause generational issues, even without any overt rebellion on the part of the child.

Realistic Goals

So what's the answer to unrealistic or dependent goals and dreams? No goals and dreams at all?

Certainly not. We need hopes and aspirations to push us forward, to challenge us so we don't stagnate or give up. Charlene Baumbach says, "These relentless pursuits fuel me to continue running the race."

The trick is to critically analyze what we want to achieve and determine how to make these goals more realistic and God-dependent instead of people-dependent.

Instead of wanting to write a best seller, I've learned I'm better off wanting to be the best writer I can be with God's help. Then only God and I come into play in pursuing that objective. Since God is always dependable, my desired result is now attainable if I am faithful. I still may not sell many books, but I can reach my goal.

Instead of seeking the praise and affection of her students, Ginny should desire to be the best Sunday School teacher she can be by God's enabling. Only she and God are needed to reach that goal, not squirmy, he's-looking-at-me six-year-olds. Pleasure in service is still possible.

Joy should seek not the best marriage but being the best wife she can be by God's grace. Again, only she and God are involved in pursuing that goal, and if Lou doesn't pull his weight or even walks out, she can still know she's done her best.

Arlene should want to be the best mother she can be with the Lord's help rather than being the poster mom for parent/child success. Reaching her goal in mothering is not dependent on a 2-year-old who may stamp his feet and scream, "No!" or a 16-year-old who continually breaks curfew. It's dependent on her faithfulness and God's constancy, and she can know comfort instead of guilt no matter how things turn out.

If no one publishes my next book, if the six-year-olds riot, if Lou is a major disappointment, and if Arlene's son grows up to be a jerk, certainly there will be disappointment and heartache. But these feelings don't have to be compounded by a sense of failure. We are no longer seeking a specific level of achievement but rather an opportunity to work hand-in-hand with God at the task He's called us to.

For the Christian, success is not in achievement but in faithfulness, in obedience.

Timing and Trust

Often, one of the difficulties we run into with our dreams and goals is that we want them fulfilled *now*. Today. Immediately. After all, the Bible says that God will give us the desires of our hearts.

Because we don't want to be like Old Testament Sarah and wait 90 years before our hopes are finally realized, we often act just like her in trying to force God's hand. Our actions might not be as extreme as Sarah's. We're not offering our maids to our husbands as bed companions so that there's a son in the house, but we are finagling and manipulating.

The result of Sarah's scheming has been centuries of conflict in the Middle East as the descendants of the maid's son, the Arabs, strive constantly against the descendants of Sarah's son, the Jews. Since our actions in forcing our goals aren't as extreme, neither are our consequences likely to touch world history for generations—but they can be just as devastating on a personal level in causing disrupted families, fractured friendships, alienated coworkers.

When the writer of Ecclesiastes says that there's a time for every purpose under heaven, he means there's a time for our hopes and dreams.

"When I was a little girl," says novelist Gail Gaymer Martin, "besides wanting to be a movie star, I wanted to write a novel. Although the idea never completely left, I thought it was just an unattainable dream." Gail went on to be an English teacher and a school counselor. "Two years after I retired, being a novelist rose in my thoughts again. A year later, I sold my first of several books. I realized that dreams can come true, but it's not our timing that counts. Dreams happen in God's time if we put our trust in Him and respond to His leading."

And if He chooses, they come to pass.

Whose Goals?

When I began to think deeply about unrealistic and dependent goals and God's timing, the Lord brought this thought to mind: What is your main desire, Gayle, to reach your own goals or to reach my goals for you?

Oops.

For God to mold me as He chooses, I may need the hurt of not being what I want to be. I may need the disappointment that makes me dependent, the pain that makes me say,

"Father, hold me close." I may need to be limited to moderate success or even to failure, and since I am by nature ambitious, the very thought of either makes me gnash my teeth.

Frequently we hear self-help gurus tell us that we can achieve anything we want if we work hard enough at it. I don't believe that is true. Just ask a defeated political candidate or a businessman who has had to declare bankruptcy or a pastor whose congregation hasn't grown in five years.

"While dreams are nice and they get us up in the morning," notes novelist Angela Hunt, "obedience to God is far more important than marching toward some distant dream that may or may not be part of His plan for us."

Obedience. For me, that has meant learning—and relearning—to pray a prayer I heard years ago: *Lord, give me the willingness to be obscure.* The very thought makes me shudder, but do I want to do what comes naturally or do I want to become godly?

I don't know the origin of that prayer, but it makes me think of a similar thought from Thomas á Kempis in his classic, *Imitation of Christ:* "O Lord, you know what is best for me. Let this or that be done, as you please. Give what you will, how much you will, and when you will."

We need to remember that Christ accomplished the Father's will for His life—and He died.

Not achievement but faithfulness.

Not success but obedience.

When people came to Jesus and asked Him to tell them

what was the greatest commandment in the Law, He answered:

> Love the Lord your God with all your heart and with all your soul and with all your mind and with all your strength (*Mark 12:30*).

He didn't say, "Write a best seller."

He didn't say, "Produce the best students" or "Model the ideal marriage" or "Live the untroubled parent/child relationship."

He told us to love the Lord with everything that is in us.

Sometimes people who love the Lord with everything in them do write best sellers, and some have great success at other endeavors.

But equally true and much less publicized is the fact that many more people who love God deeply don't write best sellers, they experience marriages that are stagnant or broken, and they rear kids who break their hearts. These are rarely the people who stand up during testimony time. We tend to hear only the "success stories"—successful, that is, in the eyes of society. Many of those glued to the pews are actually the ones who are achieving godly success—faithfulness and obedience through pain.

Other Options

"My kids love to go to a local pet store to pet the seven or eight little fluffy pups," says mystery writer Mindy Starns

Clark. "When a Pet Expo was advertised near our home, I knew the girls would love seeing the hundreds of puppies there. I decided to take them as a surprise.

"On the way, we drove past the pet store, and the kids began nagging me, 'Mom, can we stop and see the puppies? Please? Please?'

"As I drove on, I thought, *Oh, girls, if you only knew what awaits you. You're asking for a few puppies, but I'm about to give you hundreds. You want the store, but I'm about to give you the Expo.*

"I realized that is how God must feel with us sometimes. While we're begging for the pet store, He knows there's a pet expo up ahead. Trust Him. Chances are, the plans He has for us are bigger and better that anything we might have had in mind."

The catch is that He gets to pick what *bigger* and *better* mean.

Paul sets before us the alternative to unrealistic and dependent dreams, the glorious substitute for moderate success or failure, the ultimate in bigger and better.

> I want to know Christ and the power of his resurrection and the fellowship of sharing in his sufferings, becoming like him in his death *(Phil. 3:10).*

The idea of knowing Christ and the power of His resurrection is a bit daunting, but exhilarating. What a wonder to become acquainted with our Savior. What a wonder that He wants to become acquainted with us! What an exciting thing to experience His resurrection power.

But Paul also speaks of the "fellowship of sharing in his suffering" and "becoming like him in his death." Not happy thoughts, but just as much a part of the process of making us godly as the agreeable ideas.

So how do we, in this time and place, fellowship with Christ's sufferings and death? Certainly not like the Early Church with its martyrs and physical pain or like many believers risking and losing their lives for the Lord in other parts of the world today. One of the ways we might possibly fellowship with the Lord in His sufferings is through unfulfilled dreams and goals.

There is great pain in laying our hopes aside, especially when we wanted to achieve them in Jesus' name. There is a dying inside in the loss of fine desires. The heart is torn and the spirit weeps, and we lift our arms toward heaven and cry, *Father, help me. I tried. I really tried. I don't understand what went wrong. No one understands my hurt as you do. Only you can even begin to help me handle the disappointment. And you love me even though I didn't make it.*

In this way we become more dependent on the One worthy of our dependence and have our vision redirected to the truly worthy goals of faithfulness and obedience. And in the process we take another step in achieving *God's* goal for us. We become more Christlike.

Summary

It's possible that we are pursuing goals that are doomed to failure. We must set *realistic* goals.

We would do well to avoid goals that depend on others to be accomplished.

God's timing in our dreams is all important.

God's ultimate goal for us is that we know Christ, His resurrection power, and the sharing of His sufferings.

What Do You Think?

1. What are your career goals for yourself? Your spouse? Your children? Who is the most ambitious person in your family? _____

_____

_____

2. How many people are you dependent on to reach your dreams and goals? What will you do if those people don't cooperate? _____

_____

_____

_____

3. React to the following statement: "Happiness is too shallow a goal for a Christian." Read and react to 2 Cor. 4:8-9, 16. _____

_____

_____

_____

4. Read Isa. 38:1-6. What do you think of Hezekiah's prayer? Why did God answer Hezekiah so magnanimously when He doesn't answer others—probably some you know—who ask the same thing? _____

_____

_____

_____

5. Read Ps. 143:10 and 2 Cor. 2:9. What should be our ultimate goal, and how do we achieve it? _____

_____

_____

_____

How Do You Feel?

4 Worms or Princes?

Since you are going to live in your skin your whole life,
the sooner you are comfortable with it, the better.
—Diane von Furstenberg

Let me state up-front the thesis of this chapter: If you have good self-esteem, that's very nice. If you haven't, God isn't worried. He loves you anyway—and He wants to use you anyway.

The Bible presents a very clear picture of who we are as Christians, and modern psychological thought on the necessity of a good self-view isn't included. Rather, it's like using an old-fashioned stereopticon where two different, flat images become a single, three dimensional picture when we look through the lenses. Scripture presents two views of us as humans, and both are needed if we are to view ourselves properly through the life-giving lens of God's Word.

View No. 1: Unworthy Sinners

We are sinners, unworthy of God's love. The phrase from Isaac Newton's hymn, "for such a worm as I," is an accurate picture of our standing before a holy God. We may be better than our neighbor, better than almost anyone we know, but before the God of the universe, we are full of flaws and rebellion.

> As for you, you were dead in your transgressions and sins, in which you used to live *(Eph. 2:1-2).*

View No. 2: Beloved Children

But we are also beloved children of the King, ransomed at a great price.

> But God demonstrates his own love for us in this. While we were still sinners, Christ died for us *(Rom. 5:8).*

Succinctly put, we are sinners saved by grace, nothing more and, praise God, nothing less. We are wanderers who have been found. We are enemies who have been defeated by grace and taken captive by the King, transformed by His love and forgiveness into His children.

For spiritual health, we need to accept both aspects of our identity—sinner and child. Seeing ourselves only as sinners, offensive to God, denies that Christ's death was sufficient to take care of our sin. But if we see ourselves only as God's blessed children, we tend to forget the momentous sacrifice Christ made in order to bring us into God's family.

Adjust your stereopticons accordingly.

As believers, the one thing we have in common, besides our redemption, is our uniqueness. None of us imagines, thinks, speaks the same as another. To me, the most fascinating aspect about God's creation is the amazing variety of the human personality.

When I was a college student, I worked at the New Jersey shore four summers. One of my favorite pastimes was sitting on a bench on the boardwalk and watching people parade by. I was never bored because of the variety of things people said and did.

As we look, think, and act differently, so our vision of ourselves varies immensely. Some of us feel confident all the time, some of us feel confident most of the time, some of us some of the time—and some never. Given the same task, a roomful of people will show a variety of skill levels in completing that task. Those same people will view their finished products in many different ways—ways not necessarily consistent with the caliber of their work.

We all know gifted people who think they're useless, lovely people who think they're ugly, clever people who think they're dumb. How does this happen? Let's look at three influences that form our self-concept.

Influence #1: Personal Predilection or Predisposition

When my sons were small, I had an interesting conversation with my father.

"How come you never had any great problem with me or my brothers, even when we were teenagers?" I asked, looking for a clue I could carry over into my own childrearing.

Dad smiled. "It's nothing special your mother and I did," he said. "It's because none of you had a rebellious spirit."

At the time, I was not satisfied with Dad's answer because it gave me no handles to grab onto. Now, with my children grown and after years of observing other parents and their children, I think Dad was right. It was not in our natures to be troublemakers.

Certainly the nature versus nurture debate has been going on for years, and I don't have the answers. But I am convinced that certain traits are genetically coded.

One night when our adopted sons were in high school, we were driving home together. For some reason, Chip, our elder, was feeling complimentary. "Any good that I accomplish, Mom, is all because of you and Dad."

"That's nice to hear," I said, "but you know it's not true."

"Yes, it is," he insisted.

I shook my head. "You owe a lot to your birth parents, whoever they are. They passed to you your keen mind and musical ability. All we did was give you a chance to develop them."

"Nope," he said. "It's all you two."

Nature versus nurture.

Four children paint pictures. They all do a fine job, each work of art colorful and original. They even look like what they were supposed to represent.

"Let's see your work," says the teacher.

The four hold up their efforts.

The teacher looks carefully and nods. "Very nice," she says, smiling. "You all did a fine job."

Child A beams. *Yeah!* she thinks. *Did you see I used red and orange and yellow and purple and pink? It's a happy picture.*

Child B nods her head in agreement. *Yes,* she thinks, *I knew it! I did a fine job. I'm good.*

Child C looks at the teacher and at his picture. *Okay,* he thinks, *if she says it's good, I guess it is.* And he sighs, satisfied.

Child D looks at the teacher in disbelief. *No,* he thinks. *It's not a good picture. It's a terrible picture. I hate it!*

Any mother of more then one child knows what I'm saying. Any teacher knows. Any Sunday School teacher knows. Some children soak praise up like sponges. Some weigh it carefully and accept it under consideration while others are just happy not to have made a mess of things. Some have trouble accepting praise no matter how frequently and sincerely it's given.

While life experiences certainly influence strongly the way we see ourselves, the predisposition to react as Child A, B, C, or D is already present, locked in our DNA as strongly as our skin color, our hair color, or Uncle Harvey's beak of a nose.

Influence No. 2: Dissatisfaction or Bitterness

Rarely do our lives turn out the way we dreamed they would when we were children. One reason is that children tend to not allow reality, sorrow, and tragedy to intrude on their dreams. Rose-colored glasses fit best on small noses.

But real life insists on intruding, and frequently life hurts. Sometimes, the hurts are temporary and of lesser consequence—like not making it into a desired club. But sometimes the hurts are huge and life-affecting.

Why God allows His children to suffer such pain is one of the unanswered questions of life. We know that as God, He could stop the agony, but we also know that frequently He doesn't.

My friend Georgie is the victim of sexual abuse by her grandfather, and she has found that one of her biggest problems in learning to move beyond this memory is anger at God.

"Quite frankly," she told me one night, "I'm so angry at God for not protecting me that at times I don't even want His company."

Some women are angry at God for the families in which they were raised. They might not have had anyone who was physically or sexually abusive in their homes, but the verbal abuse was frequent and extremely damaging. Or perhaps the opposite situation might have been true: no one paid any attention at all.

Some women are bitter over the disappointment their husbands have been. These men have not been as successful, as financially prosperous, as caring, as committed to the Lord as their wives wish.

Some women are very upset with their looks and at the root think God should have done a better job. More bosom, less thigh, a smaller nose, fewer freckles—these are large issues to some people.

Some women are angry at God for not sending along a fine man to marry. They wanted to be a wife and mother, and they resent God's not arranging things for them. After all, He did it for friends who were clearly less deserving than they!

Whatever the cause of this root of bitterness that strangles the flower of love for God, its end result—among other things —is a poor self-image.

Influence No. 3: Believing Our Critics

Many of us have long heard dreadful messages from parents who are criticizers, bosses who are faultfinders, or husbands who are self-appointed humiliators. Some of those who maim with words are very outspoken; some are subtle. All of them cause pain.

The interesting thing is that even though we may have several encouragers urging us on to great things and only one critic, we believe the critic. We may recognize that this person has a negative spirit. We may understand that she is flawed. But for some reason, we still believe her.

The tendency is especially strong when a woman has grown up with a critical mother or father or has married a critical man. The constant drip, drip, drip of the faultfinding wears down even the most ebullient spirit and creates self-doubt.

"All I want is for my mother to say just once that I did a fine job!" Jane said with tears in her eyes. "Just once."

"Jane, she's 75," I said, feeling sad for Jane. "I don't think she's going to start being kind now."

"But she's my mother." Pain filled Jane's face. "She's supposed to encourage me. Maybe if she believed in me, I would believe in me."

Jane was 50 and had spent all those years looking for something that should have been readily available and fixating on the fact that it wasn't. She felt she had been cheated.

And she had. So has everyone who has endured relentless criticism. But the discussion of how we see ourselves can't stop here, or the bad guys win. We must understand that if we've suffered through being demoralized by a critic, had a predisposition toward feeling bad about ourselves, or if we're bitter about the way our lives turned out, it's okay.

Now, it's not okay that we were hurt or that people let us down. The inflicting of such pain is never acceptable. None of us can be faulted for feeling pain. God isn't surprised that we don't feel good about ourselves, that we feel insecure or dumb or even angry.

God does not require us to feel good about ourselves. Rather, He asks us to have confidence in Him. He doesn't ask us to "find" ourselves. In fact, He asks just the opposite. We are to lose ourselves in Christ.

> But we have this treasure in jars of clay to show that this all-surpassing power is from God and not from us (2 Cor. 4:7).

Jars of Clay

When we became believers, God could have changed us from jars of clay into lovely golden vases or silver urns or beautiful enamelwear chalices, but He didn't. He allowed us to remain clay pots—dinged, imperfect, unlovely, common.

Why did He not make us into glorious creations? Surely our instantaneous transformation into these marvelous people would have shown His great power. People would have flocked to Him for the same marvelous opportunity to become whole on the spot.

And people would have stood in line for salvation for all the wrong reasons. They wouldn't have been coming because of need or desperation or gratitude but because life would become easy and we would always be well and wealthy and pampered.

God wants it to be very clear that not only do we come to Him as dinged jars of clay, but we remain such so that it's obvious that anything we accomplish comes from His gift of grace. Not only that, but He wants us to *grow* into beautiful, glorious people. As babies don't—*poof!*—become adults, spiritual growth isn't like a magic spell. When we grow, we learn; as we learn, we *become*.

When a clay pot learns to believe God when He says He loves her, that's God at work.

When a clay pot comes to terms with anger at God and allows God to be God, that's God at work.

When a clay pot learns to believe God instead of the flawed people in her life, that's God at work.

Clay pots could never accomplish feats of that magnitude on their own. They are too human, too flawed, too self-focused.

The apostle Paul had some sort of "thorn in the flesh." What it was is uncertain, but we know Paul, a jar of clay, asked God to remove it. And we know God did not.

> Three times I pleaded with the Lord to take it away from me. But he said to me, "My grace is sufficient for you, for my power is made perfect in weakness." Therefore I will boast all the more gladly about my weaknesses, so that Christ's power may rest on me (*2 Cor. 12:8-9*).

A poor view of self may be your "thorn in the spirit." If so, you have the great opportunity to see God prove himself to you. As He was Paul's sufficiency, so He will be yours.

When I was a teenager in that quagmire of negative emotions, I found a verse that helped me see myself as God sees me. It's a verse in Jesus' prayer just before He went to the Cross. He is talking with the Father about the believers who are going to come in the future, believers like you and me.

When speaking of future believers, Christ prayed,

May they be brought to complete unity to let the world know that you sent me and have loved them even as you have loved me (*John 17:23*).

I read the verse again, and it still said the same thing. It said that God loves me *even as He loves Jesus*.

I knew all the songs and all the verses that said God loved me, but suddenly it hit me that God loved me with the same kind of love with which He loved His Son! He didn't just love me; He *loved* me!

And He *loves* you, too, with your poor self-image, your anger, your heart full of hurt from your critics.

If I were speaking to a women's group right now, I would get out a decorative basket about one foot by one foot, some Spanish moss, and a bunch of small plants. I'd take the plants, some with upright foliage, some with drooping grace, one or two with flowers, and place them one at a time in the basket. I'd put the tall ones in the back, the tumbling ones at the front to cascade over the edge of the basket, the ones with blooms where their color would show to advantage.

I would say that each plant is like a woman, different, unique, and attractive in its own way. I would remind the women that none of the plants, like none of the women, is perfect. Some of them have bare spots, some have grown too much on one side of the flowerpot, and some tend to be either a bit too unpretentious or a bit too flamboyant. But they are all special and all necessary to make a garden.

I'd finish by draping the Spanish moss like God's grace around the pots, covering the rough edges and empty spots, and I'd say, "Be the plant God has meant you to be, living the choices He has made for you without bitterness and for His glory."

Summary

We Christians are sinners saved by grace—and beloved children of the King.

Personality predilection or predisposition may be one reason we see ourselves as we do.

Dissatisfaction and bitterness with the life we have been given cause many of us to see ourselves incorrectly.

Believing what flawed people tell us instead of believing the Bible's view of us causes self-esteem problems.

Being a jar of clay gives God ample opportunity to prove himself to us in our weaknesses.

What Do You Think?

1. What do the following verses say about God's perception of you?

> Psalm 139; Luke 12: 6-7
>
> Colossians 1:13-14; Psalm 32:1-2
>
> Ephesians 2:10; 1 Corinthians 1:26-29
>
> Isaiah 43:1-3a; Hebrews 13:5-6
>
> 1 Corinthians 12:11, 18; Romans 12:5-6
>
> John 12:24-25; Romans 12:1

_____

_____

_____

_____

_____

_____

2. Who knows best what your worth is: Your parents? Your spouse? God? _____

_____

_____

3. Who will you choose to believe and why? _____

_____

_____

_____

How Do You Feel?

5   Fluttering Hearts or Rational Responses?

Feeling better has become more important
to us than finding God.
—Larry Crabb, *Finding God*

Which of the following sentences exemplifies the meaning of the verb *feel*?

I feel the president is doing a good job in the day-to-day running of the country. Or, *I feel so good when my two-year-old climbs into my lap, hugs me, and says, "I love you, Mommy."* Or, *I feel so excited about the way the Lord is blessing our church. I feel we can make a difference in the lives of the people in our community. I feel God will bless us even more as we rely on Him. I feel overwhelmed by all that has happened here.*

According to Webster, there are two meanings for *feel*, and all the uses above are acceptable.

The more common definition has to do with our emotions and traces its root to Old English verbs meaning to stroke and to flutter, even an old German noun meaning butterfly. *Feel* used in this way has to do with internal responses, fluttering hearts, and if we decide to speak King James English, quivering bowels.

The second meaning has to do with thinking, as in feeling the weight of an argument. It has to do with intellect and argument and rationale.

This distinction is important to keep in mind when we "think of [ourselves] with sober judgment" (Rom. 12:3). When we say, "I feel . . . ," do we mean that we think something, that we've used contemplation or logic or reason to come to a conclusion? Or do we mean that our emotions are telling us something, that we just know it inside?

Generally speaking, our emotional feelings are reactive, like two chemicals put together. Something happens or someone speaks, and we feel. We respond. We retaliate. We go with our gut.

In contrast, our thought feelings may be proactive, which means we take the initiative or lead. We analyze things, think about things, reach conclusions, and take action.

Emotions leave us at the mercy of each other and ourselves. Thought allows us to be in control.

For the sake of simplicity and clarity, I will refer throughout this chapter to *thought* and *emotions,* rather then to *feelings,* which is the broader category.

Several years ago, in a fit piqued over some act of discipline, one of my kids looked my husband, Chuck, in the eye and said, "I hate you."

Chuck was deeply hurt. I still remember finding him sitting on the edge of our bed looking like he'd been told that tomorrow he'd become Job.

"He said he hated me," Chuck said.

I tried not to smile too broadly, but I couldn't get too distressed. I'd already heard that line a couple times myself.

"All kids say that," I said. "It's nothing to get upset about."

Chuck just shook his head. It is more than he could fathom that a son he loved and had poured all that time and energy into could say such a thing.

"What did you say back?" I asked.

"I told him I loved him anyway."

I patted Chuck's shoulder. "Good for you. That's what all the books recommend."

"All the books?"

"On raising children," I said. "I told you it's a common

thing for kids to say. I first heard it when I refused to let one of the guys have his way when he was about three."

Chuck looked up from his contemplation of the rug. "Did it make you feel terrible?"

I shook my head. "Not really. I expected it to happen sometime. I was ready for it. After I told him I loved him and always would no matter how he felt, I told him that I expected him to say he was sorry because no one should speak to another person that way, especially a kid to his mother."

There was a knock at the door. It was our son looking miserable.

"I'm sorry, Dad," he said. "And I didn't mean it."

Emotions made Chuck reactive to the unkind words of an angry child. But thought allowed me to be proactive, prepared, above the soggy morass of gut response.

Emotions Are Good

Not that emotions are bad. They most certainly are not. Life would be pretty bland without them.

Several years ago when our church moved into a new sanctuary, Chip and his musical compatriots, Tom and Gary, wrote a song for the occasion. On dedication morning, I was filled with all kinds of wonderful emotions as I listened to Chip, his wife, Audrey, Tom, and Gary sing their song.

"I saw you smiling," Chip said later. "It seemed to me that there was this aura of motherly pride shining all around you."

I wouldn't trade those emotions—those *feelings*—for anything.

Nor the emotions when I hear those magic words, "Grandmom! Grandmom!" and see one of the grandkids run toward me, arms wide for a hug.

Nor the emotions when Chuck says, "God couldn't have given me a wife more suited to me than you."

I think God gave us emotions for many reasons, but three are worth noting:

- to warn us of danger and potential hurt, as in fear we feel when we see a speeding car
- to enable us to enjoy the good times and the good things, as in listening to Chip and Audrey's singing
- to bind us to people and causes, as in loving my sons when they were rebellious teenagers

Balancing Emotions and Thought

God also had several things in mind when He gave us the ability to think:

- to enable us to develop godly strategies to deal with our situations, as in planning how to deal with a tricky marriage or a difficult boss
- to help us grow to the place where we are willing to implement these strategies, as in beginning to build an open relationship with a mother-in-law or a coworker despite that person's criticism
- to enable us to remain committed to our strategies and relationships even after the emotion has cooled or gone, as in continuing to do our best on the job

after it has become dull or continuing to work on a marriage after the first flush of romance has waned.

What we need is a balance between thought and emotions. If we operate primarily out of thought, we will become cold, calculating, unsympathetic. If emotions rule, we're easily swayed, easily led, and life becomes chaotic.

> Then Jesus went with his disciples to a place called Gethsemane, and he said to them, "Sit here while I go over there and pray." He took Peter and the two sons of Zebedee along with him, and he began to be sorrowful and troubled. Then he said to them, "My soul is overwhelmed with sorrow to the point of death. Stay here and keep watch with me." Going a little farther, he fell with his face to the ground and prayed, "My Father, if it is possible, may this cup be taken from me. Yet not as I will, but as you will" (*Matt. 26:36-39*).

In this passage, we see Jesus feeling deep emotions. He's sorrowful, troubled, and overwhelmed. Mark says He was "deeply disturbed and troubled," and Luke says His sweat was like drops of blood. Such a reaction to the Cross is understandable because Christ knew exactly what He was going to go through physically, emotionally, and spiritually.

But—and it's a big but—Jesus made a thoughtful, controlled, proactive choice in the midst of His emotions. "Yet not as I will, but as you will."

There are times when all of us must make choices concerning situations that are loaded with emotional baggage. Our hearts pull one way and our minds pull another. We can't satisfy both. We have to decide, like Christ, whether we'll do what's right, what's best, or merely what we feel like doing.

Author Shelly Beach talked about the problem of being a mature adult who, in the right circumstances—especially around one's parents, reacts like she's still 14. "I'm continually reminding myself that the issue beneath the issue with me is usually my fear of rejection. I have to take that fear back to the truth of God's Word and who I am in Christ."

Choice. Trust the Word and do what's right. Or do what we feel like, even if it means we're acting 14.

Imagine a train made up of three cars: the engine, the coal car, and the caboose. We will label the coal car FAITH, since our faith is where we get the energy and drive to live godly lives. The other two labels we have are THOUGHT and EMOTIONS.

THOUGHT should be the engine on our life's train. It will lead us, transforming the godly energy of our FAITH into power to move forward for God. EMOTIONS will then be the caboose, definitely a good and necessary part of the train, but not the part that leads.

This ordering of our life train allows us

- to be proactive.
- to make choices based on what the Bible teaches.
- to avoid "shooting from the hip."

Author Athol Dickson says that during the period of his life when he was least balanced emotionally, "I thought I had no choice about my feelings, but that was a lie. There were always two paths before me every minute, and all I had to do was admit it and choose the upper one.

"I learned to recognize my depression and fear as a bad habit. After a run of painful events in life, one's mind becomes trained to head down familiar gloomy paths almost without thinking first. But one *must* think first. One must recognize irrational fears as the lies they are and make a conscious effort to turn to faith instead."

As Athol mentioned, our minds go where they are accustomed to going. If fear and despair and loneliness are the emotions we are used to, they are the ones we will feel until we choose to feel differently.

Whatever is true, whatever is noble, whatever is right, whatever is pure, whatever is lovely, whatever is admirable—if anything is excellent or praiseworthy— think about such things *(Phil. 4:8)*.

We're talking more than just happy thoughts here. We're even talking more than common sense. "Common sense is a gift God gave to human nature," writes Oswald Chambers. "Supernatural sense is the gift of His Son; never enthrone common sense."[1] We're talking thoughts rooted in faith, in truth, in God, and His love, in Jesus, our Savior.

"Faith," Athol reminds us, "is believing God loves me and cares about me, so He can be trusted with my future. Faith lives in joy, no matter what the circumstances. On the other hand, fear is believing God might not really love me every minute, so He might not deliver on His promises about the future.

"For me, the choice became the simple decision not to think sad thoughts. When the cloud began to settle down, I learned to recognize it before it became fully formed. 'No, I will not let you into my head!' Right at the first sign of sadness, I learned to force myself to turn to something positive instead. There is always *something* positive, no matter what, because this is God's creation, and He is good; He is love."

Not only does making these hard choices to think wisely help us as individuals to find emotional balance, but thinking things through helps us in our relationships with other people as well.

Take the situation with the girl we'll call Judy. She not only goes to your church but lives just two blocks from you, and she's having a rough pregnancy. As a result, she's having a hard time caring for her three-year-old twins, Jessi and Jeremiah. It would be easy each afternoon to have the twins over to play with your three-year-old, Emily, and then put them all down for naps. That way Judy could rest for a while without worry.

However, Judy is a critical hypocrite, and you usually just stay out of her way. Taking the twins will open you to her sharp tongue and her superior attitude on a daily basis. You know that if she's not telling you how you should be raising your kids or caring for hers, she'll be telling you what's wrong with the pastor or your Sunday School teacher or the neighbor across the street. Her faultfinding will activate your own tendency in this area, and you'll become dissatisfied with everything and everyone. And you hate yourself when you're like that!

But the Bible says we're to serve one another and help each other and love one another.

So the choice about what to do is emotions versus thought. It's "I can't get involved with her! She makes me crazy!" versus "Let us do good to all people, especially to those who belong to the family of believers" (Gal. 6:10).

If EMOTIONS are your life's engine, you will opt out of this opportunity to minister.

If THOUGHT is propelling you forward for Christ, you will care for the twins and ask God's protection from Judy's negative thinking.

But, you ask, *doesn't doing what I don't want to do make me a hypocrite? Doesn't it make me as wrong in one way as Judy is in another?*

The answer to this question lies in your motivation. Do you help Judy so everyone can see what a wonderful person you are? To prove to everyone what a fine Christian you are? Or are you caring for Jessi and Jeremiah out of obedience to God?

If our motivation for an activity or a thought choice is obedience, we are not hypocrites. We are cooperating with God and His purpose. We are obedient daughters.

Let's conduct an experiment. Turn to Eph. 4. In this passage we find that Paul gets very practical, offering many keys for everyday Christian living:

- live a life worthy of your calling (v. 1)
- be humble, gentle, patient, bearing with one another (v. 2)
- make every effort to keep unity (v. 3)
- speak the truth in love (v. 15)
- live no longer as the Gentiles (v. 17)
- put off your old self (v. 22)
- change your way of thinking (v. 23)
- put on the new self (v. 24)
- put off falsehood and speak truth (v. 25)
- don't sin in your anger (v. 26)
- don't steal, but work (v. 28)
- don't say unwholesome words but encouraging ones (v. 29)
- don't grieve the Holy Spirit (v. 30)
- get rid of anger, and be kind and forgiving (vv. 31-32)

If we wanted to list more of these instructions, we would find at least 37 additional ones in the next two chapters. When we look at these commands and all the others of Scripture, we find one very interesting thing: nowhere does it say we are to obey if we *want* to, if we *feel* like it. It simply says, "Do it!"

Doing it takes thought, not emotions.

Two Scenarios

How does this idea work out in our lives? Below are two scenarios that a lonely person might experience. In one example, the lonely person yields to her emotions. In the other, she thinks and then acts even though it's very difficult.

Helen is sad and distressed because there are no people in her life who care about her. She wants to pull the covers over her head and cry. In fact, she does that very thing quite frequently. She hates her life, and she wishes someone would come along who would be willing to be a friend, preferably a man. She doesn't know what she'd do without television, because without *American Idol* and other shows, she'd truly be alone. God has let her down big time.

Patti is sad and distressed because there are no people in her life who care about her. But because she's read in the Bible that God will never leave her or forsake her, she asks God to fill her with a sense of His presence and purpose. She's heard that He's like a friend who sticks closer than a brother, so she decides to spend time with this friend on a regular basis. She's still alone most of the time, but the overwhelming feeling of abandonment has lifted. She realizes that even though no one is encouraging her, God is still asking her to encourage others, so she asks the pastor where she can help at the church. To her surprise, she's finding friends in the people she's helping. They aren't the traditional friends she yearned for, but they are satisfying, interesting, stimulating friends. God has come through for her as she has obeyed Him, and her life becomes richer day by day.

Sometimes, what we know in our heads must override what we feel in our guts. Notice that Patti didn't feel better before she acted on what she *knew* to be God's will. She had to act thoughtfully—even while she felt miserable.

In an era of fast pain-relief medicines, most of us don't understand a concept like this. We want to feel better *now* and will do almost anything to that end. But Christ requires a little more from us because of the resources we are given through the Holy Spirit. We really can give to others when we feel empty ourselves. We can think through our problems and act in faith when emotions are still in turmoil.

Not that making these choices is easy. But they are more than possible with God's strength.

My friend Susie is a woman with a heart for God. She is also aware that she is subject to making choices by her emotions, quickly and strongly, sometimes unwisely.

"I've learned that I must take time to think," she says. "Sometimes it's as if I pick up my emotions, put them in a chair, and leave the room. Then I can pray and hear God."

Summary

Emotions tend to be reactive while thought is proactive.

God created both thought and emotion, and we are most healthy with both in our lives.

If feelings control our lives, we do what we want to do instead of what we ought to do.

If biblically grounded thoughts control our lives, we are better able to choose well.

What Do You Think?

1. When you look honestly at yourself, do you struggle against domination by your emotions? _____

_____

_____

2. When you make choices on how to deal with your husband and children, your friends, and coworkers, do you react to the situation of the moment, or have you thought about how you will behave ahead of time? (If you are in a group study, share instances when thinking and praying ahead of time made a difference.) _____

_____

_____

_____

3. Read 2 Pet. 3:1-2. Why does Peter write to his readers? How does he encourage the use of thought? _____

_____

_____

_____

_____

4. Read Phil. 4:6-9. What is Paul's suggested pattern for controlling your life and emotions? On several 3 x 5 cards

write some things that to you are pure and noble and lovely. If negative thoughts are a problem, carry these cards with you and refer to them when you feel yourself slipping into negative patterns. _____

_____

_____

_____

_____

5. Read Col. 3:1-2. How does Paul suggest we keep control of our emotions and our thoughts? _____

_____

_____

_____

How Do You Feel?

6   Pattern of Living

When I start to spin out of control,
I give up the control that reason has over me.
—Tim Wesemann, *Jack Bauer's Having a Bad Day*

Did you know that the unemployed, retirees, ministers, and women (or Mr. Moms) at home with little children share a common problem?

All are subject to depression brought on by lack of a schedule or pattern in their lives. Either no one tells them what to do or when to do it, or if they set an agenda, it often doesn't get followed. Interruptions, crises both small and large, and the demands of other people prevent schedule-keeping.

Any mother can recount tales of day after day when she accomplished nothing she had planned. The baby got sick and took all her energy, both night and day. She inherited her neighbor's three preschoolers when the neighbor was sequestered on jury duty. Her teenagers had to be carted all over the map to their various activities—and these teens apparently had taken a pledge to never belong to the same organizations.

Things are often no better at work. We know what we were hired to do, but no one ever gives us time to accomplish what we should. Little fires need to be put out with depressing frequency, and big emergencies throw everyone off schedule.

There are times when all of us could pull our hair and gnash our teeth if only we had the energy. It's then we realize there's something wonderful about order and planning: they make us think we have some control over our lives.

One of the things I like about writing fiction is that I build orderly worlds where everything makes sense. People always have reasonable motivations for what they do. The story line follows a plausible pattern. Everything that's said makes sense and furthers the story somehow. In the end, everything ties up in a satisfying and inevitable manner.

Just like real life. NOT.

Chick lit novelist Kristen Billerbeck notes much the same feelings. "I write because with four kids, MS, and all the stresses of life, I can control what happens in my fictional world, and I need that feeling of control somewhere."

The major reason we function best in orderly situations is because we are made in the image of the One who plans. From creation to the Law, from salvation to the Second Coming, we see the God of order at work.

> The plans of the LORD stand firm forever, the purposes of his heart through all generations *(Ps. 33:11)*.

When God established this world, He had a certain goal in mind: the glorious and grace-drenched salvation of those who believe in Him. Everything He has done for us, everything He has said to us, reveals this holy priority.

For us to have effective patterns, we, too, have to establish our priorities. We need to examine our strengths and weaknesses and decide what we hope to accomplish with the abilities God has given us and the circumstances in which we live. Then we must plan, because without a plan, the goal, no matter how wondrous and worthy, will not be realized. Let's look at three areas of our lives and see how planning works.

Pattern for Our Spiritual Lives

> I have set the LORD always before me. Because he
> is at my right hand, I will not be shaken *(Ps. 16:8).*

"I have set the LORD before me" means that we place Him as a counterbalance against the stress, pressure, tension, and chaos of the world. He will keep the scales of our lives stable and equalized. He will prevent us from being overwhelmed and defeated, weighed down by the heavy burdens that can fall on us.

Obviously, some of the most effective ways of setting God always before us are to worship regularly, to serve in His name, and to spend time with Him regularly and often, reading His Word and talking to Him. Just as obviously, these disciplines can be very difficult to maintain.

Several years ago a woman spoke to our church's women's fellowship on the topic of prayer. She had with her a large loose-leaf notebook.

"I have four small children at home," she said. "I simply can't find the time I'd like for my devotions every day. I know, though, that I need to spend time with God. That's why I developed this prayer notebook." She held up an ordinary book just like the ones millions of kids carry to school. "I leave the book open on the kitchen counter, and every time I look at it, I pray for the requests I write down each morning."

She flipped through the pages, words spinning past too quickly to read, but I was fascinated. She had in her hands a record of her prayers! I prayed every day, but if I had been asked, I'd have had to admit that I couldn't even remember what I prayed for yesterday, let alone last week or last year.

"Notice the checkmarks and notations on the various pages," the woman said, and I could see them as she stopped at various pages. "They are answers to prayer. Periodically, I go back through the book and write in what God has done."

Now I was really awestruck. She had a record not only of her prayers but also of God's answers. How absolutely amazing! For all I knew, God was answering my prayers, too, but I was too disorganized and too scattered to realize it.

I determined then and there to start my own notebook. I wanted to see God work, whether in answer to things I prayed for others or in the subtle but real changes in myself as He molded me to be more like Christ.

"It's not so true that 'prayer changes things' as that prayer changes *me* and I change things. God has so constituted things that prayer on the basis of redemption alters the way in which a man looks at things. Prayer is not a question of altering things externally, but of working wonders in a man's disposition," writes Oswald Chambers.[1]

The very next day I went to the store and got a binder and paper. I sharpened all my Ticonderoga No. 2s and wrote five requests on the first pristine sheet in the notebook. I prayed off and on all day for the requests. I wrote five requests the next day and the next and the next, and within a week's time made a startling discovery.

I disliked this pattern.

How unspiritual of me! was my first thought. But was it really? It was, after all, only a pattern by which I was attempting to live out a principle of the Word.

I felt that this pattern, so meaningful to the woman who spoke, stymied my prayer life rather than enhanced it. I felt it was a spiritual straightjacket forcing me into a position that was both uncomfortable and absurd.

Maybe, I thought, *I should write 10 requests. By inverse math, if she has four kids and 5 requests, then I, having only two kids, should write 10. Fewer kids equals more time available, right? I can pray longer.*

It didn't take me long to discover that I disliked writing 10 requests every day twice as much as I disliked writing five.

Lord, I prayed, *I want to see you at work, but I need a pattern that will work for me with my quirks and temperament. Help me!*

I decided that since it was the daily writing that bothered me most—which I admit is absolutely ridiculous, but there it is—I'd write all my requests down at one sitting. That way, I'd be all set. Once and done.

I began writing, and the list began growing and growing. It was as if every missionary I'd ever heard in my life came to my mind, every needy person in the whole world shouted his or her name at me. I became thoroughly weary before I'd even prayed a word.

Lord, help!

Divide them up, the Holy Spirit prompted, and I thought, *Yes, I can divide them up!* Talk about obvious.

And so I stumbled upon the pattern I have followed for many, many years. I got 3 x 5 cards, one for each weekday. I divided my huge prayer list topically, taking one category a day. Monday I set aside for anything connected with my writing. Tuesday was for my extended family. Wednesday was for friends. Thursday was for missionaries, ones I knew personally. Friday was for our church and church family. Saturday and Sunday were for whatever was on my heart.

Of course, I pray for Chuck, our sons and daughters-in-law, and our grandchildren daily. I also note crisis requests or compelling needs of family and friends in the upper margin of my cards for frequent prayer.

This pattern has changed little over the years. I now have several cards that I rotate as I pray through them and two cards I pray for as close to daily as possible. One of these special lists is composed of prodigals—friends' children who have turned from the Lord—some in great rebellion that is frightening with the potential consequences, some with a laissez-faire attitude toward the Lord that makes them nice adults but poor Christians. The second list is those who are hurting long-term through death, divorce, illness, anything that leaves scars and hurting hearts.

The interesting thing about my prayer pattern is that it may or may not work for you. You may like the notebook/daily writing idea of the women's fellowship speaker. I have friends who write lengthy prayer journals, others who pray daily with an Internet loop, and still others who have a memory that allows them to remember their requests without writing anything down. Or you may find a totally different prayer method that works well for you.

That's the catch about patterns. One pattern doesn't accommodate all believers.

One of the things I appreciate most about the Bible is that it doesn't tell us how to do things. Because the Bible is a book for all people in all cultures in all times, it can't present patterns. Rather, it teaches us principles and priorities. God in His great wisdom lets us search out our own models to fulfill His principles. He allows us to decide what best fits our personalities and our circumstances. While His principles are absolute, the patterns we develop are absolutely adaptable.

Patterns for Our Family Lives

Family living is another area of our lives greatly enhanced when we develop workable patterns as both spouse and parent.

Cherry married an engineer who is also an artist. One of the things she liked most about Randall was his sensitive, creative side. It saddened her when, after a few years of marriage and the birth of their children, he stopped painting.

"I don't need to paint," he said. "I'm happy with you and the kids. Don't worry."

One summer Cherry had to go to Florida unexpectedly

because of the sudden illness of her mother. She took the kids along and was gone almost a month. When she returned, she found her husband painting up a storm.

"It's the solitude," Cherry said, excited about solving the puzzle. "You need solitude to replenish the inner wells of your creativity."

From that point on, Cherry and the kids went to visit her parents for two weeks each year while her husband stayed home and continued to work. He also sat by streams and stared, walked alone in the woods, and spent time reveling in silence. And he gathered enough energy to keep his elusive creative streak alive all year.

Cherry told me this story and then asked my advice. "Some people at church tell me I shouldn't go away each year. It's not right, they say. I'm not being a good wife or even a considerate wife when I leave Randall behind. What do you think?"

"Does Randall mind your leaving?" I asked.

She shook her head. "He actually likes it. It's the only time the introvert in him is accommodated. Truthfully, I don't go away for myself or my parents but for him."

"The Bible talks about a good marriage in very broad strokes," I said. "That's so every culture and every couple can obey God. Your pattern is different from most people's, but that doesn't mean it's wrong. The Bible doesn't say that you may never visit your parents without your husband. It does say you should honor him and respect him, and it seems to me you are honoring him by giving him the opportunity to use all his abilities. The Bible also says you must be faithful. You are being not only physically faithful but emotionally faithful as well. You have found your pattern. Don't let others impose their patterns on you."

Maybe the following illustration will explain more clearly the uniqueness of every marriage.

Take a transparent yellow plastic report cover and draw a bride on it. Take a transparent blue cover and draw the groom. Set the sheets on top of each other, hold them to a light, and see what shade of green they make.

Every bride comes to marriage her own special shade of yellow. Every groom is his own shade of blue. Together, they create their own unique green. If they try to imitate others, their unique coloring is damaged and their potential beauty is marred. They must be themselves before God can develop their own patterns both individually and as a couple.

In *Not Your Parents' Marriage,* Jerome and Kellie Daley write:

> God intends to paint a brand new masterpiece in your marriage. He will use the same palette of colors He's always used, drawn from His unchanging character as revealed in the Bible, but every stroke will be custom fit to your unique blend of personality and calling.
>
> God will draw upon themes and examples you have inherited from your parents. . . . God will also use brush strokes that are consistent with His intention for the cur-

rent generation. . . . And, not least, God will allow each of you the fearsome privilege of holding the brush and painting what you dream into your partner.[2]

What an exhilarating, fascinating, and scary thing it is to discover the shade of green you will paint yourself.

Parenting calls for creative patterning too. Much thought and prayer are needed to determine what is appropriate for you and each of your children.

At the risk of losing half my readers, I'm going to make a confession. When my sons were still at home, I rarely asked them to make their beds. The reason? I rarely made mine.

I considered bed-making a truly futile task, certainly unworthy of confrontation. You go to all that work in the morning just to mess it up in the evening. How does that fit the principles of good time management? I do want to assure you, though, that I firmly believe in changing the bed linens regularly. And to redeem myself further, today I make my bed regularly. Maturity can show itself in unexpected ways.

I know there are women who would never leave the bed unmade, who are appalled at my laxity, who would never let a kid go to school without making his bed first. Bed-making is one way to teach responsibility.

And there we have the principle. We must teach our kids responsibility. The Bible tells us to train our children, but again it doesn't tell us how. For one woman, it's beds; for another, it's something else.

Each fall we sat around the kitchen table as a family and

divided up chores for the coming 12 months. I came to this little council with a list of possible jobs the boys could do. Chip always chose setting and clearing the table and doing the dishes. Jeff always chose the trash, the newspapers, and emptying the dishwasher. Each Saturday they both had to clean their rooms.

If they did their chores, they got an allowance. If not, no money. They could always earn extra by doing outside seasonal jobs like mowing the lawn and shoveling the snow.

"Why do we do these jobs?" they asked periodically. "It's not fair! Lots of our friends don't have to do stuff like this."

And I'd give them my three-point lecture:

- You are part of our family unit, and each part must contribute to make it work well.
- Adult life demands cooperative, responsible behavior, so you might as well learn now and save yourself trouble later.
- God asks us as parents to teach you responsibility, and you'll need it to live a consistent Christian life.

The important thing is not *what* you require of your children but that you require *something* of them. Establish patterns that fit your home and your kids. Then establish your own pattern of holding the kids accountable and then always encouraging their less-than-perfect efforts.

Patterns for Our Personal Lives

We need patterns in our personal lives as much as we

need them in our spiritual and family lives. It's so easy to become busy with family, work, and church that we take little or no time to evaluate ourselves.

> Do not think of yourself more highly than you ought, but rather think of yourself with sober judgment, in accordance with the measure of faith God has given you (*Rom. 12:3*).

Each of us has certain gifts, and we need to identify them. There are four criteria for determining a spiritual gift:

- It is something you do almost naturally.
- You enjoy doing it.
- Others respond well when you use it.
- It benefits others more than yourself.

When I was in my early 30s, I began reading Jill Briscoe's autobiography, *There's a Snake in My Garden.* I was enjoying it, but I put it aside because of some vague discomfort I couldn't identify at the time. In its place, I picked up an early book by Ann Kiemel. Shortly after, I put that down with the same feeling.

I tried to analyze what was bothering me because I admired both these women. Finally I figured it out.

Everyone these two women spoke to became a Christian (or so it seemed). Person after person responded to their invitations to trust Christ. Life after life was changed. What I was feeling was guilt because no one I spoke to became a believer. Obviously, I was doing something wrong.

I realized, though, that being upset because people were coming to Christ was—to put it mildly—foolish. After more deliberation, I came to the following conclusion: these two women have the gift of evangelism, and I do not. Instead of feeling threatened by them, I needed to rejoice that they were so effective.

Of course, I must still share the Lord whenever possible, but I accept the fact that I'll never receive the response that they do. And it's all right. I'm not them, and I have my own strengths—strengths that God has given me.

I went back to both books with this new insight and finished them, rejoicing that some are so effective in bringing people to Christ. Some plant, some water, some reap. So I'm not a reaper. Thank God others are.

As we look honestly and soberly at ourselves and consider how we can avoid emotional chaos, we need to look not only at our gifts but also at the constraints of our specific lives.

How old are our children? Can we do what we want or must we yield at least temporarily to their presence in our lives? We only get one chance with them, and we don't want to mess it up. There will be years and years for personal freedom after our mothering is finished.

Do our husbands travel a lot, or are they home every night? Do they help with the children? Are they doers or thinkers? Do they support us readily, or do they need to be convinced? Or will they never be convinced?

How much time do we realistically have right now to use

as we choose? After we finish working, taking care of the family, helping with homework, and doing laundry, do we have time and energy for outside involvement? What responsibilities do we have that no one else can fulfill?

It's important to be realistic, not fatalistic, about the limitations of our lives. All of us have people and responsibilities that get in the way of "self-fulfillment." Assess these limiting factors and determine just how truly limiting they are.

Mindy became a Christian after her marriage, and her husband, Ed, has been skeptical about her new faith. Like many new Christians, Mindy wants to be around other believers. She loves to hear the Bible taught to slake her thirst for the things of God. If she could manage it, she'd be out every night at some Bible study or another while Ed watches their three young children.

But Mindy is realistic about her situation. Even if Ed were a believer, every night out would be much too much. She is a mother, and mothering done right requires time spent with the children. And she understands that it's quite normal for Ed to want her with him instead of with people he's afraid are more than slightly strange.

"I don't go out at night," Ed says. "I stay at home to be with you and the kids. I want you to do the same thing."

So Mindy has adapted her schedule and her desires to meet her limitations. Sunday morning services and Wednesday morning Bible study give her opportunities to learn the Word, and she avoids offending her husband.

Creativity and *accommodation* are key words in finding solutions to the strictures of our lives. We're adults for a long, long time, and we don't need to experience everything today.

But what about the times when life becomes chaotic? Illnesses, deaths, layoffs, moves, divorces—when these circumstances strike, normal patterns are ripped to shreds by the demands of the moment.

When novelist Carolyne Aarson's father was terminally ill, Carolyne visited as often as possible, a two-hour drive each way. As the end of his life neared, she put her life on hold to sit vigil with her mother. As she worried about all that wasn't getting done back home, a cousin encouraged her, "God will not forget this time and will give you the grace to finish what you need to finish. For this moment He knows this is where you need to be."

When Carolyne finally returned home after the funeral, she grieved, rested, and started to stress again over all that needed to be done including the finishing of two books.

"I couldn't focus. The chaos seemed to rule my life. I stormed the gates of heaven, coming short of demanding that God honor what I had done. I felt my life was a tattered mess that I couldn't weave together any more. I needed to do something but couldn't figure out what.

"So I started small. In my quiet time I'd been reading the Bible in a year, writing a daily devotion, and reading two other devotion books. I cut back on my reading, trusting God to understand. I bought a daily planner and wrote down what I needed to accomplish each day. I prioritized these tasks and assigned each a time allotment. I did the most urgent first. When I started to panic about all the other things that had to be done, I'd look at my list and realize I'd given each task its allotted time. I could concentrate on the job I was currently doing.

"It took a few weeks, but I felt as if I were slowly making progress. Even though a lot remained to be done, I could look at my planner and see what HAD been done. I realized that control is elusive and I had to hold my days lightly.

"Now I can see that God's grace and understanding have been woven though all of this. And, as my cousin said, I did receive grace to finish what I needed to finish."

Start small would be a principle here. So would organize yourself and allow it to take time. You must find the pattern that fulfills these principles for you.

> Whatever your hand finds to do, do it with all your might (*Eccles. 9:10*).

Summary

Patterns for living are important because we are created in the image of One who plans. In our spiritual lives we want to "set the LORD always before us" in a pattern that enables us to grow in Him.

In our family lives we need to develop patterns of relating to our spouses and teaching responsibility to our children.

In our personal lives we must consider both our gifts and the limitations of our circumstances.

What Do You Think?

1. What do the following verses tell us about order and patterns?

> John 2:4
>
> Galatians 4:4
>
> 1 Corinthians 14:40
>
> Philippians 4:9

_____

_____

_____

_____

2. To establish valid patterns, we must know our priorities. As you answer the following question, it will tell you much about your priorities. *When you die and people look back on your life, what do you want them to see as your legacy?* _____

_____

_____

_____

3. Merely thinking up patterns isn't enough. Read John 17:4 and 2 Tim. 4:7. What else is required? _____

_____

_____

_____

_____

_____

How Do You Feel?

7 The Guilt Trap

False guilt is when you think you have to wait on your
husband hand and foot. Real guilt is when you don't.
—Bill Myers

When I was growing up, my mother told me, "Never
marry a man who comes home for lunch."

I figured she knew what she was talking about because my father was everything from a self-employed piano tuner to a public school teacher. When he taught school and when he worked at New York Shipyard, which was located in Gloucester, New Jersey, near Philadelphia, he didn't eat lunch at home. When he sold real estate and tuned pianos, he did.

I didn't decide to marry Chuck because of his future lunch plans, but I admit I liked the fact that even though his workplace was only 10 minutes away, he didn't come home until dinner. I had the freedom to plan my own day without having to consider his sandwich and chips.

So it was a surprise recently, while working in my office at home, when I heard our garage door go up. I glanced at the clock. It was just past noon.

Chuck rushed in. "If I hurry, I'll have 40 minutes to work on the lawn. I want to finish raking so I can put the crabgrass killer on this evening. I need to do it right away because it's supposed to rain for the next couple of days."

I nodded and went back to work. Within our mutually agreed-upon job descriptions, the lawn is Chuck's responsibility. Mine's the garden, and it didn't need crabgrass killer.

"Of course you can help me," he said graciously. "Just get a rake."

Help him? I can't help him. Procrastinator that I am, I'm too far behind in my own work. I've got to finish planning the writers' conference brochures. I've got to write some more on the book fast nearing deadline.

"But then," he said, glancing at my computer screen, "maybe you're too busy to help me." And he got the leaf eater and went to work.

Guilt, I thought. *I'm doomed to guilt! If I don't help him, I'll feel terrible, and if I do, I'll feel terrible.* My choice seemed to be which option made me feel less guilty.

My mother was right!

Types of Guilt

For the sake of accuracy, it's important to realize that there are three broad categories of guilt—*real* guilt, *continuing* guilt, and *assumed* guilt. Realizing which category a particular difficulty falls into helps us determine what to do in order to control the situation.

Real guilt, as I'm defining it, is our accountability before God for failing to keep His standards. The word *guilt* derives from an Old English word *gylt,* meaning sin. *Real guilt* exists when we commit an act against God or people that doesn't meet God's criteria of holiness.

One doesn't have to feel sorry for this wrongdoing to be guilty. A murderer may feel no contrition for his or her crime, but he or she is guilty. Guilty is something we *are,* not something we feel.

Continuing guilt is when we hang on to guilt after the cause of real guilt has been dealt with. We have confessed our wrongdoing, we have apologized for the hurt we've caused, and we have done our best to correct what we have turned on its ear through our pride or selfishness or gossiping tongue.

We feel real guilt when the Holy Spirit convicts us of our sin. We feel continuing guilt when we don't understand the full scope of the forgiveness offered us upon confession. Real guilt is a gift from God to free us. Continuing guilt is a device of the devil to hold us captive.

Assumed guilt, as I'm defining it, has to do with regret, remorse, or failure. It is a matter of misjudgment and accident rather than sin. What I was feeling when I didn't want to rake with Chuck was assumed guilt. Sin wasn't an issue, though it could have been if anger or resentment or selfishness had been involved. It was an issue of time, an issue of not being able to do it all, a regret that I was either going to let Chuck down or not get my work finished.

The wonderful thing is that Christ is there for us whether we are struggling with real, continuing, or assumed guilt. He is the Savior of sinners, the redeemer of broken lives, and the bearer of burdens.

I did go outside and ask Chuck what he wanted me to do, not because I wanted to rake, but because I felt like serving him in this manner was important. He sent me back inside, apologizing for putting me on the spot. "Go do your work," he said. "That's your first priority right now."

Yes! A clear conscience!

Real Guilt

If we are unable to admit that we are guilty of failing to meet God's standards, the Bible will thunder this truth. "All have sinned and fall short" (Rom. 3:23) leaves no room for escaping God's opinion. All have sinned, even the nice guys, the good guys, and the good girls.

Since the criterion for determining sin is God's holiness, it's not hard to see why we are guilty, whether or not we feel it.

It is because of this very real guilt and its horrific attendant separation from God that Christ became our willing and magnificent sacrifice. When we believe in Christ as the Savior who took all our sins upon himself when He was crucified, our very real guilt is forgiven. Our position in Christ makes us guiltless in God's eyes.

In him and through faith in him we may approach
God with freedom and confidence *(Eph. 3:12).*

What a wonderful truth! We cannot be spiritually condemned as guilty because in Christ we are guiltless. God is not our judge but our Father.

Therefore, there is now no condemnation for
those who are in Christ Jesus *(Rom. 8:1).*

When we are guilty of breaking human laws, punishment decided by our legal system is the standard way of dealing with the crime. We may be fined, serve so many years in jail, or be assigned a designated number of hours of community service.

Many times, the acts that the state finds reprehensible are

the same deeds God holds us accountable for. The difference is that where the state punishes, God through Christ forgives.

> If we confess our sins, he is faithful and just and will forgive us our sins and purify us from all unrighteousness (*1 John 1:9*).

While salvation and forgiveness make us sinless in one sense, we still do sin. There is a thought in Romans that I frequently pray because I know my tendency to excuse myself and to minimize my guilt. I pray that "sin might become utterly sinful" to me (Rom. 7:13). In other words, I want the Holy Spirit to teach me when I am offending God, when I am truly guilty. God may no longer be my judge, but He is my Father, and as His loving child, I desire to please Him.

Continuing Guilt

It is all too easy to accept the truth of our forgiveness intellectually but not apply it emotionally, leaving us feeling guilty for sins long ago forgiven. "Why?" asks novelist Harry Kraus. "Because we seem to be wired with an amazing capacity to forget the magnitude of God's love for us. The problem isn't the size of the Cross to fill the gap between my wickedness and God's holiness; it's my perception of the size of the Cross."

We get tangled in the consequences of our sin or in the idea that we have to forgive ourselves or we need to deserve being forgiven. "Anything I do to gain His forgiveness," Harry reminds us, "including feeling guilty so I'll deserve it, takes grace out of the equation and makes our confession or guilt feelings penance."

In Revelation, John refers to Satan as "the accuser of our brothers" (12:10) who accuses them before God day after day. He also accuses us day after day in our minds and our hearts.

"Remember that terrible thing you did? Remember? You think God could love you after you did *that*? Yeah, yeah, so He forgives you. Or so He says. But come on. How could He forgive *that*? You are so unworthy. How could He ever use you? How could He ever trust you again?"

And because we feel terrible, because we feel guilty, because we feel unworthy, we listen. We agree. We wallow in grief and self-recriminations. Sure, we manage to push our bad feelings out of our minds for periods of time, sometimes long periods. Then boom! It all rushes back. We forget that the guilt that we want relief from has, as Harry says, "been perfectly taken care of by the work of the Cross."

Let's rethink a few things so we're not led by our emotions but the truth of the Word. Let's remind ourselves of things we know but all too often fail to make practical.

First, we are unworthy. We've already talked about the fact that in spite of our unworthiness, God loved us enough to sacrifice His Son for us. What we have to remember is that when He says, "I have loved you with an everlasting love" (Jer. 31:3), He is saying nothing less than the absolute truth. And this love is perfect. That means that His love is stable, never changing. It cannot lessen. It is never withheld.

If our lack of worth is not an issue to God, why do we let it be such a great issue to us? We have to choose. Will we believe our feelings or the truth of God's great love?

Second, we *were* guilty. Note: *were*. The moment we asked for forgiveness, we were forgiven, and as a result, we are no longer guilty. Christ, our great guilt bearer, bore all our offenses in His own body on that terrible tree.

> Let us draw near to God with a sincere heart in full assurance of faith, having our hearts sprinkled to *cleanse us from a guilty conscience* and having our bodies washed with pure water (*Heb. 10:22*, emphasis mine).

Real conviction of wrong behavior, of sinful behavior, is the work of the Holy Spirit in our hearts to bring us to confession. Guilt that continues long after confession is not from God.

Writer Dandi Daley Mackall notes,

"God doesn't waste energy being vague. Conviction from the Spirit is pointed, like a sword, specific. When I get those vague, depressing guilt feelings that I'm a crummy person and an awful Christian, I ask God to be specific and show me the actual sin if these feelings are from Him. Otherwise, I've learned to ignore these feelings."

There is another type of continuing guilt worth noting, and it's wrapped in the psychological phrase "forgive yourself."

In many of our lives, there is a particular sin we committed—often many years ago. This sin is especially reprehensible to us, and we have confessed it so many times we've lost track. Every time we remember it, the pain and shame it caused—and causes—and the distress we knew and know, we confess. Our hope is that finally, eventually, we will feel cleansed.

I had such a sin in my life. Every time I thought about it, I'd pray, *O, Lord, forgive me. I'm so sorry I did it. Forgive me.*

One day I realized a specific truth. *The first time I had asked God to forgive this action, He had done so.* It was gone, washed away in the grace-filled crimson flood that flowed from Calvary. I was the one holding on.

Since it isn't in God's character to play games with us, He wasn't sitting up in heaven poking me with the pins of conscience, making me squirm with guilt every time I remembered. It was the enemy accusing. By contrast, God had given me forgiveness and His gracious care. He had liberated me from the burden of guilt while I, foolish woman that I can be, allowed myself to be bowed with the weight of something that wasn't even there any more.

> It is for freedom that Christ has set us free. Stand firm, then, and do not let yourselves be burdened again by a yoke of slavery *(Gal. 5:1).*

When I kept asking for forgiveness for the same sin over and over, I was saying that Christ's sacrifice wasn't sufficient for me. He could not set me free. What I did those years ago was too terrible for Him to handle. His death atoned for all the sins of the world except this particular one of mine, and I had to keep pleading with God over it.

Of course, I didn't mean to devalue Christ's death by holding on to my assumed guilt, but I was doing so nonetheless. Instead of Christ increasing and me decreasing, it was the other way around. I was adding myself to the work of the Atonement.

But how, someone may ask, can I recognize when I am being accused by the enemy as opposed to when the Holy Spirit is convicting me about something I honestly need to correct?

There are two tests we can apply to make this determination:

1. Have we confessed our sins to God, admitting our guilt and asking His forgiveness? If the answer is yes, then the feelings that persist are accusations.

2. While Satan seeks to drive a wedge between us and God, the Holy Spirit, on the other hand, seeks to reveal our sin to us so that we can restore our damaged relationship with our Father. Satan is divisive. The Holy Spirit is a healer.

In order to silence the accusatory voice within me, I got down on my knees and prayed, *God, I realize you forgave me years ago, the first time I came to you about this sin. You chose to do that for me even though I didn't deserve it. It is not of you that I still feel guilty over this issue. I want this day to be a watershed in my Christian life, a day I can look to every time I remember this sin, every time the enemy accuses me. Because of Christ's death and based on the promises of the Word, I know I am forgiven and free.*

Now, whenever I think of this issue, I recite 1 John 1:9 and remember my forgiven state. Instead of great regret and embarrassment, I rejoice in the graciousness of a God who doesn't keep accounts against us.

Assumed Guilt

Assumed guilt, as I'm defining it, is the guilt we take on over situations in our lives that aren't sin-related or sin-caused, things like failure, regret, and circumstances.

Failure

Pat had quite a collection of plants, all given to her when her husband died. She carefully watered them every week. And every week as she did so, she felt full of guilt.

How is it, she'd think, *that I can keep these stupid plants alive, but I couldn't keep Tom alive?*

Finally, distressed and haunted by the emotions the plants caused, she threw them all out.

"I knew what I was feeling was illogical, but I kept thinking I should have been able to do something for Tom, something to make him better or something to bring him back. The plants symbolized my failure."

Failure. How we hate it. We hide it from others. We deny it to ourselves. Often, because of our culture and a you-can-do-anything-you-set-your-heart-to mind-set, we assume that failure is an offense against God.

The truth is that many fine Christians fail in business, in school, in relationships. While it is accurate that sin may lead to failure in any of these areas, it is equally true that failure can come where there is no sin. In fact, a desire to do God's will and honor Him may be very much in the heart of the person who falls.

When such a failure occurs, it is good to ask yourself: By whose standards have I failed? My family's? America's? My own? God's?

It is very possible that when we fail, we have disappointed our families and ourselves, but that doesn't mean we have disappointed God. His desire for us is *not* success. It is, as the Westminster Catechism says, that we love Him and enjoy Him forever. It is that we become like Christ. Our failures do not make us unacceptable to God or make Him love us less— just as our successes do not make us more attractive to Him or cause Him to love us more.

God's purpose for us can be reached in failure as well as in success. For failure, like illness or bereavement, can be His tool to develop us and make us more dependent on Him. Failure makes us vulnerable and teachable. It may well be one of His greatest gifts to us.

Regret

If failure is frequently mistaken as something over which we should feel guilt, regret is often mistaken for guilt itself. We did something that had bad consequences, and we're ripped up inside. What we did wasn't wrong, but somehow it turned out wrong. People were hurt, property damaged, and we were devastated or discouraged, but we didn't mean for anything bad to happen.

Certainly we apologize and we try to make restitution if appropriate, but in the sense of offending God, we are not guilty. We don't need to seek His forgiveness. Rather we need to ask Him for a double measure of His strength, His wisdom, and His ability to repair the damage and damaged.

> Come to me, all you who are weary and burdened, and I will give you rest (*Matt. 11:28*).

There is a sense in which regret can be a good thing. It can be the motivation to do better next time. We're distressed or embarrassed by the way things turned out, and we don't want it to happen again, so we learn how to do what must be done in a better manner.

When a woman tries to become a published writer, she submits her manuscript to an editor for consideration. This work will either be accepted or rejected. If it is rejected, the would-be writer is filled with regret. It wasn't good enough. She wasn't good enough.

There's no wrongdoing involved here, just ignorance or dearth of training or lack of talent. But there is regret, which, at this point, will cause the writer either to decide she is not good enough and choose to give up or push her to learn to do better. If regret does the former, the would-be writer will remain a wannabe and will live with the regret of a goal not reached. If the rejection makes the writer study more, write more, learn more, then the regret has a very positive effect.

Circumstances

Another way we find ourselves feeling unnecessary guilt is when we are the victims of small, everyday circumstances. We can't be at two games at the same time, and one kid is going to feel rejected. We can't be room mother this year because our ill grandmother has come to live with us, but our youngest doesn't understand. We won't be teaching Sunday School this year because we need some time off, but the superintendent doesn't take our resignation well. We won't be going to Mom's for Christmas this year because as a family we need Christmas in our own home, but Mom is so upset she cries. We won't be at Back-to-School Night because we have to work, and we fear that both the kids and the teacher think our priorities are wrong.

Life is full of hard choices, and there's no way we can make everyone happy with our decisions. After we pray, we just consider all sides of an issue and choose, asking God to help fill in the holes that we can't. Certainly, if we can, we make it up to the hurt party in some other way, but if we can't, we can't. It's nothing to feel guilty about; it's just life.

Summary

There are three types of guilt: real, continuing, and assumed.

Real guilt is our culpability for failing to meet God's standards. Guilty is something we are, not something we feel.

Continuing guilt comes when we let our bad feelings over our actions rule us rather than the fact of God's forgiveness in Christ.

Assumed guilt is when failure, regret, and circumstances are mistaken for real guilt.

Jesus forgives our sins, redeems broken lives, and bears our burdens.

What Do You Think?

1. Scripture urges us to confess or acknowledge more than just our sin. What do these verses tell us?

> Romans 10:9
> Matthew 10:32
> 1 John 4:15
> 2 Corinthians 9:13

_____

_____

_____

_____

_____

2. When we confess our sins, what great gifts does God give us?

> Psalm 32:5
> Colossians 2:13

_____

_____

_____

_____

3. Read Psalm 130. What promises are here for those experiencing real guilt? _____

_____

_____

_____

4. If we suffer from assumed guilt, from failure or remorse or pain, what do these verses offer as hope?

> Psalm 7:1
> Psalm 18:1-3
> Psalm 32:7
> Psalm 46:1
> Isaiah 25:4
> 1 Peter 5:7

_____

_____

_____

_____

_____

_____

How Do You Feel?

The Guilt Trap

Controlling Emotional Chaos

I've always found it far easier to name problems—to tsk-tsk over them—than it is to correct them. However, just putting a name to a difficulty doesn't reduce it. We may know now what to call our problems, but controlling these areas is as great an issue as it ever was. It's time for specific, practical means of developing emotional consistency.

The concepts we are about to discuss, when applied and accompanied by dependence on God, can make a great difference in the quality of our Christian lives. We are going to examine:

- Repentance and confession
- The old self-new self concept
- The need to practice godly living
- The place of contentment
- The absolute necessity of daily commitment

Lord, teach us what we need to learn, and give us the wisdom and courage to act on this knowledge.

8 Cleansing Confession

Man is born broken. He lives by mending.
The grace of God is glue.
—Eugene O'Neill, *Traveling Mercies*

I grew up in New Jersey, a state where you must be 17 before you can get your driver's license. For me, this was no great hardship in spite of the fact that just across the Delaware River in Pennsylvania, 16 was the magic age.

However, that extra year apparently was difficult for my older brother, an honor student and student council president. One day, when our parents were out, he couldn't wait any longer. Since Mom and Dad wouldn't be back for quite a while, he took our other car for a little spin. He didn't go far; just a short drive around town. Unfortunately for him, Mom and Dad got back sooner than expected, and they were watching out the living room window when he pulled up out front.

"I never saw anyone go as pale as he did when he saw our car in the driveway," said Mom with a gentle laugh. "Talk about being caught red-handed!"

As I recall the story, no one said anything to my brother about his little drive for a couple of days. Remember, this was a kid who rarely did anything wrong and who hated to disappoint. My parents decided that stewing in his guilt was a more effective punishment for him than any lecture or social restrictions or other quick resolution. It must have worked. He never took the car again.

To my brother's credit, he never tried to explain or defend himself. He was wrong and he knew it. Guilty.

We are all guilty. Maybe we haven't taken our parents' car, but we've done something we shouldn't have. As my brother was caught in his "crime" by Mom and Dad, so we are observed in our wrongdoing by our Father who sees and knows everything. Incredibly, even when we know we're guilty, many of us still try to talk our way out of our actions as if God didn't realize what we had done or as if He should have a different set of standards for us.

"Hey, everybody cheats on taxes. It's not such a bad thing to do. I mean, it's not murder or anything, and why would God be paying attention to me anyway? He's got better things to do."

"I know you asked me not to say anything about the difficulties you and your husband are having, but Janny wanted to know what was wrong. This way, she could pray for you too. But don't worry. I told her not to tell anyone else, and I'm sure you can trust her."

"The cashier gave me back a ten instead of a one for change. You know how tight things have been for me recently. Every little bit helps. God won't care, and it is only a ten. Boy, this is sure my lucky day!"

It is absolutely imperative for our emotional health and consistency—to say nothing of our spiritual development—that we are honest with ourselves and others. The issue is not *whether* we have broken God's standards in a big way or a little way. The issue is that we *have* broken it, period. And we must acknowledge it.

A few years ago, our son Jeff was preparing for the opening day of fishing season. He got his rod and reel ready, and he bought a good supply of worms, which he put in the refrigerator overnight.

Ashley, then three years old, was curious about what was in the worm container. Jeff opened it and showed her the worms crawling around in the dirt.

Ashley got so excited she started dancing. "Oh, Daddy," she said. "You've got sidewalk snakes!"

In truth, no matter what Ashley calls a worm, it's still a worm.

In the same way, no matter what we call an action that falls short of God's standard, it's still sin.

I don't think there is any cure for being a worm, but there is a remedy for believers who are entangled in sin, no matter how terrible, no matter how trivial.

The first part of the cure is repentance; the second is confession.

Repentance

Repentance is basically changing one's mind, and we can repent of all types of things. We can repent about buying that red and orange dress. What were we thinking? We can repent about quitting our jobs. The work may not have challenged us, but it beat having no paycheck. We can repent about our nasty thoughts toward someone. After all, feeling this way lowers me to her level. For the purpose of this book, however, we will use the narrow theological definition of *changing our minds about our sin.*

We need to change our minds about cheating on our income tax, acknowledging that we broke the law.

We need to change our minds about sharing private information, realizing we are guilty of gossip.

We need to change our minds about the $10.00 mistakenly given us by the cashier, agreeing that keeping that money was stealing.

Frequently, it's sorrow that causes us to acknowledge our wrong behavior. Paul writes about "godly sorrow," the sadness we experience when the Holy Spirit teaches us that we have offended God (2 Cor. 7:10). While Paul mentions that this sorrow leads to salvation, this distress also leads believers to restored relationship with the Father.

Godly sorrow may cause us to pray, *O, God, I feel so awful about what I have done. I can't sleep at night, I can't eat, and all I want to do is cry. It seemed like such a good idea at the time, but I know now it wasn't. It was wrong. Forgive me.*

David knew this godly sorrow when he wrote:

My guilt has overwhelmed me like a burden too heavy to bear. My wounds fester and are loathsome because of my sinful folly. I am bowed down and brought very low; all day long I go about mourning *(Ps. 38:4-6).*

It is also possible for God's kindness to bring us to repentance (Rom. 2:4). We do something that offends God, and He still blesses us, still cares for us, still loves us. We are overwhelmed by His kindness.

Then we might pray, *O, God, you are so good to me. I am so ashamed of the way I have disobeyed you and hurt you when all you do is love me. Forgive me for my wrong actions.*

John recognized this overwhelming kindness of God when he wrote:

This is love: not that we loved God, but that he loved us and sent his Son as an atoning sacrifice for our sins *(1 John 4:10).*

It's been my observation that we all repent in different ways—some with tears, some dry-eyed, some with upset stomachs, some with improved digestion. It's a small matter of temperament and background. The emotion we may or may not feel is not what is important; the *changing of our minds* to bring our thinking in line with God's is.

Confession

Repentance and confession are closely related, but there are differences worth noting.

As we can repent of any number of things, so we can confess any number of things. We can confess our real ages when someone tells us we look younger. We can confess that we love someone, whether to the loved one or to another. We can confess that we took the last chocolate chip cookie, and we don't feel the least bit guilty. For our purposes, we will use the biblical definition of repentance: *saying the same thing as God* or *agreeing with God.*

Because we have repented or changed our minds about how we look at things, now we confess our sins or agree with God not only that certain behaviors are wrong, but also that we were wrong to do or think them.

We now agree with God that cheating on our income taxes is wrong.

We now say the same thing as God about passing on gossip. We now agree that keeping that ten was theft.

Just as repentance is experienced with a variety of emotions, so is confession. We may cry in sorrow or we may stoically admit that we missed the mark. We may feel shame or we may not. We may race to the altar and publicly admit our wrong, or we may kneel by our beds at night and whisper our confession to God's ears alone. We may feel great relief to get the weight off our backs or we may feel nothing, resting on the promises of Scripture for the knowledge of our cleansing.

Remember principle and pattern? The principles of repentance and confession are straight from the Word. The pattern of embracing these principles will be yours alone, but repentance and confession are where we must begin if we want to get and keep some semblance of control of this squiggly, slippery thing we call life. We have to examine ourselves and our actions and ask some very hard and possibly painful questions.

Lord, where am I falling short?

Father, are there people I have hurt or am hurting?

Is my tongue a weapon or a balm to those I know?

Lord, am I the model of Christ I should be to my children?

Holy God, are my thoughts pleasing to you or full of jealousy and malice or impurity and unhealthy desire?

Lord, will you make sin exceedingly sinful to me?

The wonderful thing is that we needn't be afraid in this process. God has promised us forgiveness ahead of time. Before we acknowledge any sin whatsoever, God set in motion what Philip Yancey calls the scandal of unconditional grace. God is always ready to forgive us; we are the ones who hold back.

Several years ago I was on a parent-teacher task force at the kids' elementary school. All the other schools in the district had similar panels. Our task was to examine the school, the curriculum, and the school district and then pass on both our concerns and ideas for correcting any weaknesses.

We met several times, and we came up with a list of things that concerned us—things like lower teacher-student ratios, more reading programs, better vocational training for kids who were not college bound. However, we couldn't come up with many practical ideas on how to correct these concerns without spending a lot of money that the district didn't have.

Just as the task force outlined the problems that kept our schools from being all they could be, you and I have problems that may disrupt and limit our lives. But—and it's a very big but—unlike the task force that couldn't correct the problems in public education, we as believers have the wherewithal to define and correct our life problems. Where the task force had limited resources and limited opportunity to make a difference, we have at our disposal the very power of God in the person of the Holy Spirit to enable us not only to acknowledge our shortcomings but also to change as we need to.

As we've already seen, these changes begin with repentance and confession, but they don't end there. Coming to God's conclusion about sin does not immediately revamp one's whole life. However, it begins the process.

Summary

We must acknowledge our problems and sin if we hope to correct them.

Repentance is changing one's mind about an action or thought.

Confession is agreeing with God about one's action or thoughts, the result of changing our minds.

Repentance and confession are the beginning steps in the process of getting control of our emotions.

What Do You Think?

1. Read Psalm 38. What caused David, that great man of God, to repent? What did he confess? What was the result in his life of harboring sin? _____

_____

_____

_____

_____

2. If you change your mind and agree with God, what do you expect to happen? _____

_____

_____

3. Read 1 John 1:9. What does this verse say about the wrong things you have done or the good things you have left undone? What about the things you aren't aware of? _____

_____

_____

How Do You Feel?

9 The Put Off—Put On Principle

Our first task is not to forgive,
but to learn to be the forgiven.
—Stanley Hauerwas, *The Peaceable Kingdom*

Tammy woke up Monday morning before the 6:30 alarm rang, a very unusual experience for one who thought bedtime should be between midnight and 1:00 and rising between 8:00 and 9:00. She lay quietly beside Hap, eager for the day to begin.

Lord, she thought, *today's going to be such an exciting day! I can't wait to see how you help me. Today I become a new woman.*

For some time now, Tammy has known that she had to do something about her mouthiness. Somewhere, somehow, she had stopped speaking nicely to the people she lived with, the people she loved most.

Granted, four sons aged 2, 4, 6, and 8, and a husband who acted like a 10-year-old half the time were enough to make most women sound off—if only as a means of self-preservation. But she knew she did more than sound off, and she'd never read about self-preservation in the Bible.

"Darren, you're such a bully! Leave your big brother alone. Who do you think you are, you little animal? I ought to give you to the zoo! Those lions would shape you up in no time."

"Carlton, you turn that TV off before I wring your neck! I told you to go to bed, and I mean it! Off, off, off, you terrible kid! What did I ever do to deserve you?"

"Barton, you shut your mouth before I shut it for you! I don't want to hear any complaints! Just once I want you to be a good boy and do as I ask without me having to throw a fit. Come on, surprise me once before I have to visit you in jail. That's where bad kids end up, you know."

"Alvin, you can be so dumb! Look where you're walking, why don't you? You've got two good eyes in that empty head of yours, haven't you? There should be plenty of room for them because you obviously have no brain!"

Tammy shivered as she thought of all those nasty things she'd said to her sons. In reality, she loved them dearly, but she never sounded like it. It was easier to yell. *Her* mother had always yelled, and she still struggled with the hurt of her mother's tirades.

"I'll never be like that when I have kids," Tammy had told Hap when they were dating. "I hate the way she talks. I hate the way she always makes me feel. I promise never to speak like that to you or any kids we might have."

Yet, here she was, inflicting the same pain on her own boys. Most days she made her mother sound like Cinderella's fairy godmother.

Yesterday in church she had listened to the pastor speak on the tongue. It was James 3:9 and 10 that convinced her she must do something:

> With the tongue we praise our Lord and Father, and with it we curse men, who have been made in God's likeness. Out of the same mouth come praise and cursing. My brothers, this should not be.

O, God, she prayed. *I've been so wrong! Help me to not speak so unkindly. Help me to not be so mean to my kids and Hap. Help me to not be like Mom!*

Now she was ready to change. When the alarm went off, she got up right away.

"Are you sick?" Hap asked. "Don't you feel well?"

"I'm fine," Tammy said defensively. "Why do you think I'm sick? Are you saying I look terrible or something?"

"You just got out of bed without complaining and griping. You always make a scene about getting up."

"I don't like mornings," Tammy explained for the millionth time, her patience wearing thin. Would the man never listen?

Hap smiled sardonically. "Tell me about it."

Tammy put her hands on her hips and scowled. "Look, Mister, you're no ray of sunshine at 6:30 yourself."

"Of course not," Hap said, his smile gone. "I live with you."

With that he slammed the shower stall door behind him.

"That's right," she fumed as she put the toothpaste on her toothbrush. "Run out on our discussion."

"Discussion?" he yelled over the sound of rushing water. "Discussion? We haven't had a civil discussion in years!"

"And whose fault is that?" she yelled back.

"Not mine, sweetheart," he said in a tired voice. "Not mine."

"So it's all my fault, huh? Of course! I might have known. Blame it on Tammy. Then your conscience will be clear. Well, I'll tell you something, Hap! I'm not going to fight with you anymore." She stamped her foot for emphasis. "I'm turning over a new leaf." She thought about the tone of her words in the five minutes since she'd risen. "Starting tomorrow morning!"

She stared at her reflection in the mirror. How had she blown her good intentions so quickly? How could it have happened when she was so sincere? When she meant so well? When she had asked the Lord for help?

The Positive Replacement

Tammy experienced disappointment and failure because she grasped only part of the process of godly change in our lives. She understood the negative part of the equation. She wanted to *not* speak unkindly and combatively. She understood that such speech dishonors God. But if she didn't say ugly words, what did she say? She couldn't keep silent for the rest of her life.

Tammy never thought to develop a positive *replacement* for the negative pattern she wanted to abandon. When she thought only of putting off her nasty speech patterns, she created a hole, a void, a vacuum.

In life, as in nature, a vacuum cannot exist. Something will always rush in to fill the empty space. When the crunch comes, what rushes in is our old behavior or old habits because that is what we know.

When Hap got sharp, Tammy had only a vacuum of good intentions to respond with. Back scurried her old pattern of speech. The known, no matter how much it is hated, will win over a vacuum every time.

> You were taught, with regard to your former way
> of life, to put off your old self, which is being corrupt-

ed by its deceitful desires; to be made new in the attitude of your minds; and to put on the new self, created to be like God in true righteousness and holiness
(*Eph. 4:22-24*).

These verses show us the three-step process we need to
follow in order to successfully change our bad habits.

1. We "put off" our old sinful self. In other words, we recognize what's wrong, repent, confess, and determine to stop.

2. We "become new in the attitudes of our mind." We
think about how we will go about making the necessary
changes. We decide what good action will replace the bad behavior we are giving up.

3. We "put on" the new self. We replace our wrong actions and attitudes with the godly behaviors we've previously
thought about and chosen.

The rest of Eph. 4 explains clearly how we are to act on
these steps.

Therefore each of you must put off falsehood and
speak truthfully to his neighbor, for we are all mem-
bers of one body (v. 25).

1. Stop telling lies.

2. Agree with God that lying is wrong and telling the
truth is right.

3. Start telling the truth because we are believers and
should help each other.

He who has been stealing must steal no longer, but must work, doing something useful with his own hands, that he may have something to share with those in need (v. 28)

1. Put off stealing.

2. Agree with God that stealing is wrong and working is right.

3. Begin working so you'll have the means with which to share with others.

Do not let any unwholesome talk come out of your mouths, but only what is helpful for building others up according to their needs, that it may benefit those who listen (v. 29).

1. Put off saying things that hurt.

2. Agree with God that speaking unkindly is wrong and speaking kindly is right.

3. Put on helpful speech, encouraging speech, in order to build others up.

Get rid of all bitterness, rage and anger, brawling and slander, along with every form of malice. Be kind and compassionate to one another, forgiving each other, just as in Christ God forgave you (vv. 31-32).

1. Put off all forms of anger and bitterness.

2. Agree with God that speaking or thinking with animos-

ity is wrong and showing kindness, compassion, and love is right.

3. Put on compassion and forgiveness because in Christ God has forgiven you.

Godly Thinking

Suppose Tammy had understood the full biblical equation for changing. Suppose she had understood that not only did she have to stop speaking unkindly and critically, but she also had to plan how to speak kindly to build her family up. She had to think of nice things, pleasant things, encouraging things. Suppose she understood that she needed to learn to think as Christ thinks about the people she lives with. How might her morning have been different?

"Are you sick?" asked Hap when he saw her get out of bed so early. "Don't you feel well?"

Out of habit a defensive answer rose to Tammy's lips, but she knew she had to say something positive, not nasty.

God, give me nice words.

"I feel fine," she said. "I can't say morning's my favorite time, but I'll be okay."

Hap nodded in understanding as he climbed into the shower. "I'm not wild about mornings either."

Tammy smiled at herself as she brushed her teeth. Up five minutes and already she avoided an angry retort.

Thanks, Lord.

"By the way," yelled Hap over the roar of the water. "Do I have an ironed shirt for today?"

Tammy froze. An ironed shirt. She opened her mouth to say accusingly, "Why didn't you tell me yesterday that you were wearing your last one?" Instead she bit her lip. Such a response was at best a weak effort to transfer responsibility.

She peeked into the closet. No ironed shirt. She hurried to the laundry room. No ironed shirt. She sighed and looked into the washing machine. Lots of shirts, none even dry, let alone ironed.

She pulled one out and threw it into the dryer. With any luck it would be dry by the time Hap finished shaving. If she pulled it out right away, maybe it wouldn't need ironing.

Suddenly a loud and anguished "Mom!" pierced the air.

"What's wrong?" Tammy went flying to the rescue.

"He kicked me, Mom! He kicked me and knocked over my Lego building!" Alvin, her oldest, was standing in the middle of the room, pointing at the offender, two-year-old Darren.

Biting back a "Shut up, Alvin! You'll wake the dead!" Tammy said calmly, "Are you telling me that the baby kicked you so hard with his sleeper-covered feet that you're in great pain?"

"Yes," said Alvin. "I mean, no. I mean . . ."

Choosing not to say, "Darren, you little animal, are you being a troublemaker again?" Tammy picked the baby up. "Come on, Sweetie; let's get some Cheerios. We want to leave Alvin alone so he can rebuild his beautiful building."

You may feel such a scenario sounds too easy to be true,

and you may well be right. My point, though, is that when Tammy learned to make conscious choices by applying the entire put off-put on pattern, her quality of life improved dramatically.

But let's say she had responded to Alvin with one of her tart rejoinders. What should she do? Give up until tomorrow?

No. What she should do is ask God's forgiveness, ask Alvin's forgiveness, and try again. She may need to ask repeatedly for the Holy Spirit to remind her of what God thinks of these people in her life. At first she'll fail a lot out of habit, but if she perseveres, she'll fail less and less, succeed more and more. In time, speech seasoned with grace will be her normal way of talking, though it's important to acknowledge that she will never be perfect—nor will you and I.

The following dialogue written by novelist Ethel Herr reminds us that when we fail in spite of our good intentions, our Father is always there.

> "And how many times may I slip and fall over this same cliff before you tire of reaching down to pick me up? Surely you have your limits, Lord."
>
> *"My child, as many times as you stumble and then raise your hand up to me, I'll be right here reaching out to grasp and pull you up. Redeeming you is what it's all about, for you are precious beyond words to me."*

What is the action or pattern you need to change in your life? Do you, like Tammy, yell too much? Is your speech clever at the expense of others? Do you envy your neighbors for their financial ease, resulting in your looking down on your spouse for not making more? Do you have unhealthy sexual thoughts about one who isn't your husband?

As we wrestle with these unworthy habits, Ethel suggests we must remember God's perspective: *"Simply confess to me that you have sinned once more, that you are more sorry for the grief of my heart than for the shame of your imperfection."*

Summary

Just recognizing sinful things we want to change in our lives isn't enough. We must adopt the pattern of putting off and putting on.

1. Putting off wrong things

2. Renewing our minds to agree with God about how we should do things and

3. Putting on the right or godly behavior to avoid a vacuum effect

This put off-put on principle should apply to everything we think about as well as what we do.

What Do You Think?

1. What habit or behavior has the Holy Spirit been convicting you about? If you put it off, what godly behavior should you put in its place? _____

_____

_____

_____

2. Read Colossians 3:5-10. What instructions are we given here? Why should we change? _____

_____

_____

3. Read Romans 12:2. What is the result of renewing your mind? _____

_____

4. When Paul finishes writing the examples of put off-put on in Eph. 4, he wrote 5:1-2. What two instructions did he give to those of us who are renewing our minds? _____

_____

_____

_____

5. In these same verses we see what putting on a life of love may require of us because of what it required of Christ. What is your response to such a cost? _____

_____

_____

_____

How Do You Feel?

The Put Off—Put On Principle

10 Persevering Practice

Character is what a man is in the dark.
—D. L. Moody,
The Wycliff Handbook of Preaching and Preachers

We had a black-and-white cat named Bugsy who thought he was the world's greatest hunter. He loved to stalk squirrels and rabbits and birds. He refused to let the fact that he had no foreclaws deter him. Instead he relied on speed and surprise.

Because he was a well-fed animal, Bugsy rarely showed an interest in eating his prey. His pleasure was mainly in the chase.

Many times I looked out back and saw him hiding behind a tree or a stump waiting for a gray squirrel to forget he was there. To my knowledge, the squirrels were never that foolish. If Bugsy went for them, they'd run up a tree until they were just out of reach. There they stopped and delivered a loud and probably profane lecture.

While he had trouble with gray squirrels, Bugsy reaped other prizes with his constant practice. I heard him "murp" one day and came into the family room inside the sliding doors to find a baby rabbit cowering in a corner, completely unharmed but scared to death. I finally coaxed it to run into Chuck's slipper and, after carefully closing Bugsy in the house, took the slipper and the rabbit to the woods and left them there. By the time Chuck came home, the rabbit was gone and the slipper was back in the closet.

One night Bugsy brought in a flying squirrel still very much alive. I have no idea how he managed to catch it, but as soon as he loosened his hold on it, it began tearing around the house. We all watched and were properly impressed when it leaped off the top of the cellar step and flew down to the basement, rounding the bend in the steps very gracefully. Jeff was finally able to catch the little creature in a box and take him outside.

Unfortunately, Jeff wasn't here the summer Bugsy brought in a live chipmunk. Chuck and I tracked him to the back bedroom, then couldn't figure out how to get him out of there. He kept climbing up into the mechanism of the sofa bed we kept there.

After several aborted and totally graceless tries, we finally got a box on top of him and slid a piece of stiff cardboard under him. We were barely out the back door when the cardboard separated from the box and the little guy was gone, hopefully never to return.

I am convinced that the main reason Bugsy had such success in spite of his lack of claws is that he practiced and practiced. For every success, there were many misses, many gray squirrel lectures. But if he hadn't worked so hard, he'd have had all misses.

The same idea applies to developing emotional consistency. We need to practice, knowing there will be failures, but continuing to work at godly living until the successes are more frequent than the failures.

> Anyone who lives on milk, being still an infant, is
> not acquainted with the teaching about righteousness.
> But solid food is for the mature, who *by constant use*
> have trained themselves to distinguish good from evil
> (*Heb. 5:13-14, emphasis mine*).

Practicing Godliness

I find it interesting that the writer of Hebrews says it is the mature believers who practice. It is the mature who by constant use have trained themselves to distinguish good from evil. It is the mature who persevere until they make the put off-put on pattern a way of life. It is the mature who recognize that renewing their minds is a spiritual skill that requires time and commitment.

"In all things, God is present," writes Mark Buchanan in *Your God Is Too Safe*. "Whether we notice Him or not is a matter of vision, attentiveness, alertness—practice." We all need to develop what Mark calls "a steady vigilance in godly things."[1]

If He had wanted, God could have made us completely godly in our living patterns at the moment we trusted Christ. He could have. But as we all know from experience, He didn't. Instead, He wants us to practice and grow and mature a step at a time. He wants us to persevere, to learn a steady vigilance in being godly.

Perhaps it's a greater miracle than instant sanctification that in this world men and women choose to live holy lives simply because they love God and want to please Him. Perhaps it is a greater miracle that they struggle against their natural tendencies, practicing, practicing, practicing godliness in order to be salt and light.

We're used to the idea of athletes training hour after hour, performing a specific skill over and over when it doesn't count, so that when the competition finally does occur, when it finally does matter, they are prepared. Those in the military also practice skills over and over so that in the heat of combat, their responses are automatic.

When I was writing the novel *Allah's Fire* with Chuck Holton, a former Army Ranger, we had Chuck and his family as well as our editor join us at our vacation place in Canada. One evening Chuck showed us how to disarm someone who had a long-barreled weapon and someone who had a handgun.

"All you do is step between them and the gun," he said, demonstrating on my husband who held his arm out like he had a weapon. Quick as anything, Chuck had his back against my Chuck's chest and his hand on the imaginary gun. "Then when they pull the trigger, which they will do as an automatic reflex, they shoot their own comrades."

"All you do . . ." Right. All you do after hour upon hour upon hour of practice.

In the same way, we as believers should be practicing, studying the Word, talking with the Lord, listening to those gifted in opening the Scriptures, making godly choices in the small, daily things of life. Then, when the inevitable crunch comes, we will be ready to handle it in a manner that honors God.

When athletes train, they have their coaches to guide them and instruct them. The more gifted the coach, the better the athlete. The more teachable the athlete, the better his or her performance will be.

We have a coach, too, who will guide and instruct us. The Holy Spirit delights in teaching us how to become more consistent. He rejoices in training us to be godly, in tutoring us to discern good from evil, in strengthening us for the trials ahead. It is our responsibility to be teachable, trainable believers.

As we commit our hearts to God and as the Holy Spirit leads us, we grow and we change. An acronym for "practice" will help us remember what's involved in these changes.

P rocess

R epitition

A ction

C ommitment

T edium

I ntegrity

C ommonality

E xcellence

Process

When our boys were small, each summer we had memberships to a pool in the area. The pool fielded a swimming team, and the boys wanted to be on it even though they couldn't get from one end of the pool to the other when they started and even though they had to practice every morning in the chilly air and water.

At one early competition Jeff was chosen to swim the breaststroke in the eight-and-under category. I was delighted for him because he was so pleased. He took off as fast as he could, and he had the lead when one of the officials, walking down the side of the pool beside the racers, raised his fist and pointed at Jeff.

"DQ," the man said.

The child was disqualified because his kick was incorrect for the stroke. Somewhere along the line a coach was supposed to teach the kids the proper kick, but it had never gotten done.

At the end of the meet when the 18-year-olds swam, it was another story. The training *process* and the year-in-and-year-out practice showed quite clearly.

Christian living is a *process,* too, not a static experience. Today, we are not what we want to become, but we are also not what we were. We are advancing slowly, developing our own Christian histories, resting more on the Lord, learning step-by-step how to honor Him. We are in process.

Repetition

I am amazed at the discipline first-rate athletes have. They are willing to spend countless hours doing the same skill again and again, seeking a better swing, a greater body extension, a more fluid movement, or a fraction of a second.

Christian living requires the discipline of *repetition* too. Each day we commit ourselves to God. Each day we seek His will. Each day we make choices for His glory, not ours. Each day we say, "He must become greater; I must become less" (John 3:30).

As an athlete cannot afford to grow careless about the basics, neither can we. When we rebel against *repetition*, we are in deep spiritual trouble.

Action

After a life of having dogs as pets, we adopted three cats.

As I compared them to the wonderful dogs in my past, I concluded that they differ most dramatically from dogs in acting on command. Or, I should say, *not* acting on command.

Ask anything of a dog, and he'll try to make you happy, even if he hasn't the faintest idea what you want. He'll run in circles, bark, try to kiss you, or sit in your lap. A dog is an *action* animal.

A cat, on the other hand, will sit and stare at you no matter how elementary the command. He feels no need to please you, no need to do something merely because you want him to.

While I hope that I would have a little more dignity than most dogs in my effort to obey my Master's commands, I would hope I never develop a catlike hostility to action and practice. I want to say as Christ, "I have come to do your will, O God" (Heb. 10:7).

Commitment

There is one thing besides eating that our cats were committed to, and that was protecting the sanctity of their home turf. A black-and-white cat suddenly began to visit us, and Bugsy, Stooge, and Fluffy were anything but pleased. In the cold weather when the sliding door was closed, our guys would sit on the inside and this interloper would sit on the outside, and all four would howl and shriek and growl.

When warm weather came, and the cats were outside a lot, they physically defended their territory. One day I found Fluffy and this cat-stranger locked in mortal combat with

Bugsy running around making guttural noises. Stooge was hiding safely inside, no stooge he.

I broke up the fight by touching Fluffy and the other cat on their backs and startling them so that they each let go. The strange cat took off with my cats chasing him.

We believers don't wrestle—usually—with a physical enemy as our cats did, but we certainly do engage daily, moment-by-moment, in spiritual warfare. We need to be absolutely *committed* to our God and to practicing holiness if we have any hope of being victorious.

Tedium

I have noticed through the years that no matter what responsibility I have been given, and no matter how much I may enjoy that responsibility, part of the job has always been tedious. Keeping my files up to date and my desk clear are, to me, tedious chores. So are folding the wash and putting away the groceries. So are bed making and preparing the garden for winter.

The Christian life is full of tedious moments too. Cooking another meal for another new young mother, teaching another Vacation Bible School for the 30 millionth year, preparing another Sunday School lesson for kids who rarely listen, washing up after a church dinner. After the first hundred times, these jobs lose their charm.

Christ probably found it tedious walking back and forth across Palestine under the hot Middle Eastern sun, teaching the same thing again and again to people who didn't hear. Yet

He did what He was supposed to do, *tedium* or no. So must we.

Integrity

Several years ago, when I flew home from a writers' conference, my mom was to pick me up at the airport. I sat on a bench in the pickup zone reading as I waited for her arrival. When she came, I quickly tossed my things in her trunk.

We were getting out of the car at her house when I realized I didn't have my purse. I remembered setting it besides me on the bench, but I couldn't remember picking it up.

Mentally kissing my credit cards and money good-bye and dreading the complications of canceling everything and replacing it all, I went inside.

My dad's first words were, "Hi, Gayle. Lose something?"

A young woman had seen me get in Mom's car and drive off without my purse. She picked it up, took it home with her, and called to say she had it. Chuck and I stopped at her home in Philadelphia the next night to get the purse and thank her profusely.

Whenever I think of *integrity*, I think of this young woman. And I pray that I, as one who names the name of Christ, will be as honest and upright as she.

Commonality

Many years ago I used to write a weekly column for our local paper. I would tell about the right-around-home things that happened in our family—Jeff's third birthday party, Chip's first grade Halloween party with me as a homeroom mother, Chuck's pulled ligaments, my locking myself out in my bathrobe when no one was home. At the end of each column I'd have a spiritual parallel and a verse or a prayer.

I was completely surprised at the positive response to these little pieces. People even started asking Chuck, "Are you Gayle Roper's husband?" I especially loved this since we live in Chuck's hometown and people are always asking me which of the Ropers I'm related to.

The reason for the response to the columns was that I wrote about things all families experienced. My kids said funny things; their kids said funny things. I made a fool of myself; they made fools of themselves. *Commonality*.

There's *commonality* in our Christian experiences too. As we practice godliness, we struggle with similar things, like establishing regular times with the Lord or speaking only what encourages or keeping the TV monster under control or determining how much freedom is enough for our teen or deciding our financial responsibility to our church. And we all need the Lord's strength to keep on keeping on.

Excellence

Several years ago, when people first started asking me to autograph books I had written, I realized what an ego-inflator these requests were. It would be very easy to begin thinking that what I wrote was the last word in great writing.

I determined two things back then:

1. If what I wrote in a book or article was not based on

the Word of God, it was no more than an opinion and as such could and should be readily ignored.

2. To remind myself where I must stand to have any real value to my readers, I began signing what has become my life verse, Col. 3:17, after my name. "And whatever you do, whether in word or deed, do it all in the name of the Lord Jesus, giving thanks to God the Father through him."

As I practice doing everything in the name of Jesus, I have no choice but to strive for *excellence*. Anything less is simply not acceptable.

There is a song by Kelly Willard that spells out clearly what practice is all about and what it accomplishes.

> *In a hidden valley just over the hill*
> *A young shepherd boy surrenders his will*
> *As he lifts his voice in praise to his King*
> *Only the lambs will hear and follow as he sings.*
>
> *Hidden valleys produce a life song*
> *Hidden valleys will make a heart strong*
> *Desperation can cause you to sing*
> *Hidden valleys turn shepherds to kings*
>
> *In a hidden valley a faithful one leads*
> *No one looking on, he cares for their needs*
> *For he knows the one who tries the heart*
> *So he is steadfast and content to do his part.*

Hidden valleys produce a life song
Hidden valleys will make a heart strong
Desperation can cause you to sing
Hidden valleys turn shepherds to kings

In a hidden valley a leader is born
He has faced the fierce and weathered the storm
So with humble heart and love for his God
He becomes royalty with just a staff and rod.

Hidden valleys produce a life song
Hidden valleys will make a heart strong
Desperation can cause you to sing
Hidden valleys turn shepherds to kings. *

* "Hidden Valleys" by Kelly Willard, copyright 1991 Willing Heart Music. All rights reserved. International copyright secure. Used by permission.

Summary

Practicing godly living over and over when no one's around trains us for the inevitable crunch.

We practice until there are more successes in godly living than failures.

God could have given us instant holiness when we became believers, but He chose to make us practice instead.

It's the practice—the hidden valleys—that turns us into kings.

What Do You Think?

1. In his Epistles Paul records his prayers for the various New Testament churches. What does he pray for believers and how does practice relate to these requests?

> Ephesians 1:15-21
>
> Ephesians 3:14-19
>
> Philippians 1:9-11
>
> Colossians 1:9-12

_____

_____

_____

_____

_____

2. What area in your own Christian life needs practice? What plan of action will assist you as you practice? _____

_____

_____

_____

3. Read Hebrews 6:12. How does this verse relate to practice? _____

_____

_____

How Do You Feel?

11 Learning Contentment

We were driving home from church one Sunday morning several years ago when Chip, then 12 going on 20, asked, "Why do you always have to tell me what to do? It's not fair."

I looked at my son, slouched so low that he was practically sitting on his neck. It being Sunday, I knew what was bothering him. "We all go to church, Chip. That's just one of the rules in our home."

"You don't have to make rules for me. I can take care of myself! I can't wait until I get out of this house!" (To offer hope to those of you who are currently in this situation, Chip is now a pastor. But in junior high. . . .)

"You want to be free to go where you want when you want? To hang out with the kids you want? Go to bed when you want? Wear what you want? Stay home from church when you want?"

His face brightened when he realized I understood. "That's it!"

I nodded. "As soon as you can pay your own rent, buy your own food, and afford the gas for your own car on which you pay your own insurance, you'll be ready to be on your own."

He looked at me, appalled.

"And of course there's buying and washing your own clothes and paying your own health insurance and buying your own movie tickets."

"But," he said with all the sincerity and naïveté of a kid, "I only want the good parts!"

I think many of us look at contentment as "the good parts." When we are at ease, when we are comfortable, when we have enough—whatever that is—we will be content.

When life allows us to be relaxed and as fear-free and self-satisfied as a cat curled before a fire on a winter's night, then we will be content. When we finally earn enough to do whatever we want or go wherever we want, then we will be content. When we finally marry the man of our dreams and have wonderful, cute babies who grow up to be wonderful, cute adults without rocking the family boat, then we will be content.

Scripturally, though, that definition doesn't work. It's much too American and land-of-plenty-ish. The Bible is a cross-cultural book. Any definition for biblical contentment must apply in the droughts and political chaos of Saharan Africa, the oppressive governments of Islamic lands, and the cyclones and tsunamis of Southeast Asia as well as the prosperity of the United States and Canada.

The whatever-I-want definition also doesn't work because it's much too I-call-the-shots. We forget that God is the one in charge and that He has His own idea of how things should work for us.

> "For I know the plans I have for you," declares
> the LORD, "plans to prosper you and not to harm you,
> plans to give you hope and a future" (*Jer. 29:11*).

The trouble we have is that God's plans require giving up our plans and trusting Him for all that is good—and giving Him the right to define *good*.

Novelist Camy Tang says:

Contentment was such a punishing issue when I was

single. What seemed to come so easily to some girls was a constant war zone in my heart. I couldn't deny that I wanted a boyfriend, I wanted a husband, and I couldn't get my heart to desire Christ instead, even though I wanted to. I couldn't be happy and content in my singleness.

At this point, Camy was defining *good* her way.

"Then one day," she goes on, "I realized that contentment wasn't about me. I was spending so much time focusing on my longings and feelings and struggles, when all the time my discontent was supposed to make me focus on Christ. I hadn't realized that my heart wasn't completely, totally given over to Him.

"After that realization, contentment was still a daily battle, but my heart was a lot stronger, and my spirit felt more at peace. Not completely content—but soothed, and at rest."

One of the things I love about Camy's story is the acknowledging of the daily battle, the need for her to *practice* her commitment, building her spiritual muscles as she wrestled.

Keys to Contentment

Since contentment is dependent upon several things, we're going to talk about four: sufficiency, obedience, learning, and farsightedness.

Sufficiency

To be content we must agree with God that He and what He has given us are *sufficient* for His purposes for us.

God's definition of *sufficiency* challenges me. I don't understand how starvation fulfills God's purpose for some while garbage disposals full of leftovers satisfies His plan for others. I do know that God has placed each of us in the country, culture, and family in which we were born, and therefore His plan for us somehow involves the ease or difficulty of our circumstances. I often wonder if it's harder to follow God in plenty where you have everything and more or in want where all you have is Him. Whichever, our responsibility is to trust Him whatever our situations.

And we can trust Him because by His very character God is all-sufficient. From His unending well of enough He pours upon us sustaining waters sufficient for His purposes for us.

> And God is able to make all grace abound to you, so that in all things at all times, *having all that you need,* you will abound to every good work *(2 Cor. 9:8, emphasis mine).*

Obedience

To be content we must obey God and follow Him no matter what the cost. Sometimes such obedience is easy because His will is very obvious.

> It is God's will that you should be sanctified; that you should avoid sexual immorality; that each of you should learn to control his own body in a way that is holy and honorable . . . Make it your ambition to lead a quiet life, to mind your own business and to work with your hands, just as we told you *(1 Thess. 4:3-4, 11).*

Sometimes God's will is harder to discern. Should we move? Should we change jobs? Should we take a job? Should we spend that money on the new rug that we need or give it to church? Should our kids stay in Christian school or go to public school?

No one can answer these questions and countless others for you, and no one can tell you which answers are God's will for your life. Certainly there are many who will be only too happy to tell you what they think you should do, but only you can decide. However, you can make wise choices if you have been living in obedience. Are you reading the Word? Are you fellowshipping with believers? Are you practicing godliness? Are you putting off and putting on? Have you prayed about the decision you need to make?

If the answer to these questions is yes, then you make what you consider to be the wisest call and trust the Holy Spirit to open or close doors. The real issue isn't whether or not you move. The real issue is how you live wherever you live.

Of course, sometimes we make decisions despite what we know to be wise and godly. Because we want something or think we deserve something, we set out to have it our way. We manipulate and finagle and refuse to ask God for His leading. When we make a mess of it, of course we want God to fix it.

> You are still worldly. For since there is jealousy and quarreling among you, are you not worldly? Are you not acting like mere men? (1 Cor. 3:3).

When we act like, in our case, mere women, deep serenity and contentment are impossible. When we obey God, the tension of our mutiny disappears, and we are ready for the third key to contentment.

Learning

> I am not saying this because I am in need, for I have *learned to be content* whatever the circumstances. I know what it is to be in need, and I know what it is to have plenty. *I have learned the secret of being content* in any and every situation, whether well fed or hungry, whether living in plenty or in want *(Phil. 4:11-12, emphasis mine).*

When Paul wrote this letter to the Philippians, he was a prisoner in Rome. When he wrote about being well-fed or hungry and living in plenty or in want, he wasn't exaggerating. He was admired and lauded on one hand and persecuted and hated on the other. Yet whatever the circumstance, he agreed with God that he had sufficient resources for God's purpose for him.

I first found Paul's thoughts on contentment in my teens. A personal situation was eating at me, and I was becoming bitter. One morning I read Paul's wise words, and life literally was never the same. From then on these words have been a challenge to me in difficult situations.

When I was 26 and had a total hysterectomy and would never be able to have children, this verse challenged me to *learn* to be content with the unexpected path God had laid out for me. I didn't come out of the anesthesia saying, "Praise God. I can't have children." I mourned my loss and cried my tears. I challenged God's wisdom. I had to *learn* to trust Him in this circumstance.

When I entered a black period in my writing life where I went five years without a sale, again I prayed that I would learn to be content even if God's purpose for me was apparent failure. I didn't wake up each morning saying, "I look forward to another day with no sale." I didn't go to bed each evening saying, "Oh, good, another day with no sale." Rather, I wrestled with my ambition and desire to succeed. I had to *learn* to be content even if I never sold another thing.

Some days this learning can be a minute-by-minute grabbing of emotions and giving them back to God. "Here, Lord. I can't carry them anymore." It's not a denying of sorrow or disappointment or loss. It's giving them to God to hold for us so we don't need to shoulder the overwhelming burden. Here we learn contentment *in God's care* in our circumstances as opposed to in the circumstances themselves.

At other times, contentment lingers sweetly, and life feels good. We lie back in our emotional hot tubs and go, "Ah. Thank you, Lord."

The fact that contentment is something to be *learned* reminds us again that the Christian life is a process. It's like a child who first learns to count, then tackles simple arithmetic, moves on to math and algebra, and eventually to trigonometry and calculus.

For it is: Do and do, do and do, rule on rule, rule on rule; a little here, a little there *(Isa. 28:10)*.

In other words, learn. Practice.

Farsightedness

To be satisfied with what God has provided for us, we have to see with eyes that look beyond today, beyond our present problems. The promise of Christ's return and of heaven are given to us to foster this long view of things.

The New Testament is full of promises about the future because life for first-century Christians was so hard, so full of persecution. After his classic description of the Lord's return in 1 Thessalonians, Paul concludes, "Therefore encourage each other with these words" (4:18).

Now a man came up to Jesus and asked, "Teacher, what good thing must I do to get eternal life?"

"Why do you ask me about what is good?" Jesus replied. "There is only One who is good. If you want to enter life, obey the commandments."

"Which ones?" the man inquired.

Jesus replied, "'Do not murder, do not commit adultery, do not steal, do not give false testimony, honor your father and mother,' and 'love your neighbor as yourself.'"

"All these I have kept," the young man said. "What do I still lack?"

Jesus answered, "If you want to be perfect, go, sell

your possessions and give to the poor, and you will have treasure in heaven. Then come, follow me."

When the young man heard this, he went away sad, because he had great wealth *(Matt. 19:16-22)*.

This poor young man was unwilling to take the risks involved in finding contentment, and for him the risks were great. He had to give up his wealth, his lifestyle, his autonomy, his everything, and he was loath to do so.

He would not agree with Christ that God and His provisions could be sufficient.

He would not be obedient to Christ's words.

He would not give himself any time to learn contentment as Christ's follower.

And most of all, his vision of the *future* was completely colored by his *now*, by his wealth, by his own ideas of what was best for him.

Doesn't he sound just like us?

I confess that farsightedness is the most difficult part of contentment for me. I have a hard time working up great enthusiasm for being with the Lord either by His coming or my going. My life is too pleasant.

I look out my back door at the lushness of my flower garden with its marvelous shades of ruby, lavender, fuchsia, and emerald, and I like it right here.

I lie snug in my warm, dry bed, cuddled against my loving husband, and listen to the rain pelt the roof and tumble down the drain, and I like it here.

I visit with my sons and daughters-in-law, I watch my grandchildren grow straight and true, I relax with a good book in my hand, I enjoy a dinner out with Chuck, and I like it here.

While in a sense God has blessed me because "the boundary lines have fallen for me in pleasant places" (Ps. 16:6), in another sense I have lost the edge and excitement of appreciating God's future for me. I have more in common with the rich young ruler than I like to admit.

Summary

Contentment is agreeing with God that He and His provisions for us are sufficient for His purposes for us.

Obeying God is a prerequisite for contentment.

Contentment is something we can learn whatever our circumstances.

A contented Christian is farsighted, loving the promises of Christ's return and of heaven.

What Do You Think?

1. Is there an area in your life where you find yourself disagreeing with God about His provision for you? Or His provision for someone else? _____

_____

_____

_____

2. *Webster's New World Dictionary* defines *contentment* as being satisfied. From a natural, human point of view, is

contentment possible? How does a Christian's understanding of contentment differ from the world's? _____

_____

_____

_____

3. Read Prov. 19:23. What is necessary before a person can rest content? _____

_____

4. Can contentment and ambition coexist? Contentment and progress? Contentment and dreams and goals? Is contentment the same thing as complacency? _____

_____

_____

5. Read 1 Tim. 6:6-10. How does this passage remind you of the rich young ruler? What lessons are especially pertinent to you? _____

_____

_____

_____

How Do You Feel?

Learning Contentment

12 Rooted Commitment

> For a little reward men make a long journey;
> for eternal life many will scarce lift a foot
> once from the ground.
> —Thomas à Kempis, *Imitation of Christ*

Aha! I finally knew what I would do for my four sisters-in-law for Christmas. I'd give each of them a bulb garden that would bloom in January and February. Every time they looked at its lush colors in the middle of winter's dark cold, they would be reminded that spring would burst upon them in a couple of months. Every time they smelled the heady fragrance of the narcissus, they would think, *How clever and kind of Gayle to give such a thoughtful gift*.

I knew that's what I'd think if I got a gift that nice.

I ordered the crocus, tulip, tête-à-tête daffodil, and paper narcissus bulbs from one of the best mail-order gardening companies. I carefully read all that I could find on how to create and raise healthy bulb gardens. I bought the soil recommended and pots to contain these marvelous gifts.

I planted the bulbs in November as advised, taking care that they each were placed at just the right depth in the pots. I put them in the garage, which was both dark and cool. I watered them only as much as I was told. And I waited.

The pots I had gotten were clear plastic, and when I checked on the progress of my gardens, I could see the root systems developing. I was fascinated by the hairy white tendrils pushing their way through the soil, and I was confident I'd have a superior product to give. When tiny sprouts poked their tender, pointed heads out of the soil, I knew all was in good order.

Then I noticed that the little sprouts weren't growing taller, and their color was no longer a healthy, sturdy green. Soon every one was a crispy, very dead brown.

I think it was the clear pots that were responsible for the deaths of my wonderful gifts. It couldn't have been me, right? The week before Christmas I was out frantically looking for some wonderful somethings to replace my deceased flowers.

Now for my analogy. After all, I must get some value out of those dead plants.

So then, just as you received Christ Jesus as Lord,

continue to live in him, *rooted* and built up in him, strengthened in the faith as you were taught, and overflowing with thankfulness *(Col. 2:6-7, emphasis mine)*.

Rooted in Christ

When I think of what our relationship with Christ is to be, I think of those wonderful root systems my bulbs developed. I can see in my mind's eye the young shoots growing down into that soil, burying themselves in it, drawing life from it.

That's the way we need to bury ourselves in Christ, rooting ourselves firmly in Him. As a strong root system anchors a plant in the ground, protecting it from winds and storms, so burrowing deep in Christ protects us from the potential ravages of life's storms, storms that are guaranteed to come.

A good root system also provides nourishment to a plant, pulling water and nutrients from the soil and through capillary action passing these life-giving necessities to the entire plant.

Similarly, our roots buried deep in Christ—the Bread of Life and the Living Water—nourish us, enabling us to grow and blossom in even the most extraordinarily difficult circumstances as well as in the pleasant, sunny places.

My analogy breaks down at this point, as all analogies eventually must. My bulb gardens never grew due to the limitations of their gardener. But we have the Master Gardener tending us, and He knows exactly how to care for us, how to encourage us, how to insure we bloom with the sweet fragrance of Christ.

This is what the LORD says: "Cursed is the one who trusts in man, who depends on flesh for his strength and whose heart turns away from the LORD. He will be like a bush in the wastelands; he will not see prosperity when it comes. He will dwell in the parched places of the desert, in a salt land where no one lives. But blessed is the man who trusts in the LORD, whose confidence is in him. He will be like a tree planted by the water that sends out its roots by the stream. It does not fear when heat comes; its leaves are always green. It has no worries in a year of drought and never fails to bear fruit" *(Jer. 17:5-8).*

Which are we? Are we the bush in the wastelands, depending on our own strength? Are we that stunted tree dwelling in the burning desert or in the barren salt lands, fixated on what we don't have instead of what we do have in Christ?

Or will we be a tree planted by the bubbling springs, our thirst quenched, our leaves always green? Will we be the sturdy oak or graceful willow by the rushing stream, our confidence in God so strong that we don't fear or worry, at least not very often and we're working on that?

When we ask these questions cloaked in the illustration of wizened bushes in wastelands and strong trees by the stream, the answer seems so obvious. None of us wants to be stunted and deformed. We all want to prosper and grow, stretching to the sky. We want to provide shade to those who need it and produce fruit to enrich those who pass by.

However, asked straight out, stripped of all picturesque language, the question is harder to answer.

Are we willing to be so rooted in Christ that we trust only in Him, choosing always to do His will, opting always to follow His lead, deciding always to yield our todays and tomorrows to Him?

Core Issue

The question of commitment, of becoming wholly God's woman, is the core issue of learning to be emotionally consistent. It is from this basic decision that all our godly options flow.

We can learn how to set godly and reachable goals when we become willing to do things His way instead of ours.

When we say, "Lord, I'm yours," we accept that God values us and will use us no matter how lacking in self-confidence we may be.

When we make our commitment to Christ, we make the choice from careful thought, not an emotional high. Then we revel in the joy He sends.

We are able to develop strong, godly patterns when we say, "Lord, I'm not only willing to do it your way, but I *want* to do it your way. Teach me."

We learn to deal with real and assumed guilt when we open our hearts and minds fully to Christ, the forgiver of sins and the bearer of burdens.

I can do everything through him who gives me strength *(Phil. 4: 13).*

Well, if commitment to the Lord is so profitable for ordering our lives and making us content, why do we struggle so with giving God our all? There are several possible answers to this question, but I'd like us to look at the cares of life and the "dailiness" of living as major culprits that mitigate against commitment.

The Major Culprits

It's not that we don't love God. We do. We talk to Him whenever we have time. We keep our Bibles on our bedside stands, ready when we have a spare minute for our devotions. We even have a notebook to write down prayer requests. It's just that time is so limited, and there are so many other things, so many good things that must be done. We're caught in the tyranny of the urgent.

It's not that we're angry with God or overtly rebellious. We think God's principles as presented in the Bible are very wise and practical. We have great admiration for people who live by these principles. It's just that applying them takes more concentration and energy than we have or are willing to extend right now. But someday, maybe when we're older, when the kids are older. . . .

And it's not that we don't recognize there are needs all about us. We most certainly do, and we agree that the church should be getting involved in hurting lives with the healing messages of salvation and servanthood. It's just that our present priorities are our families and our jobs. When these situations ease up, the kids leave home, or our husbands get promoted, then we'll think seriously about all that God asks of us.

Do these thought patterns sound familiar? They're ages old. We're certainly not the first ones to be distracted from our highest goals by merely important goals.

> King Solomon, however, loved many foreign women besides Pharaoh's daughter—Moabites, Ammonites, Edomites, Sidonians and Hittites. They were from nations about which the LORD had told the Israelites, "You must not intermarry with them, because they will surely turn your hearts after their gods." Nevertheless, Solomon held fast to them in love. He had seven hundred wives of royal birth and three hundred concubines, and his wives led him astray. As Solomon grew old, his wives turned his heart after other gods, and his heart was not fully devoted to the LORD his God, as the heart of David his father had been. He followed Ashtoreth the goddess of the Sidonians, and Molech the detestable god of the Ammonites. So Solomon did evil in the eyes of the LORD; he did not follow the LORD completely, as David his father had done (1 Kings 11:1-6).

Many of Solomon's wives and concubines were acquired because it was politically expedient for him to have links with the surrounding nations as a means of keeping hostilities at bay in the region. Apparently Solomon convinced himself that peace was primary, and if keeping it meant bending the laws of God concerning intermarriage with godless nations, well, so be it. God would understand.

Of course, once Solomon had all these women, he was responsible for their care and for the care of his children by them. It appears that one way he showed his concern for them—and one way he kept peace in the seraglio, I imagine—was to allow these foreign women to keep their gods. Again, expedience led Solomon to disregard another of God's absolute commands, this one to keep Israel clean of idols.

For the wisest man who ever lived, Solomon had a remarkable ability to deceive himself. In the name of amity, he abdicated his spiritual leadership and responsibility to his people.

Solomon's most serious step away from God, the God he still claimed to love and the God who allowed him to build the Temple in spite of his sin, was when the influence of his foreign wives led him to worship their gods, even the loathsome Molech to whom child sacrifices were offered.

Did you notice that Solomon's spiritual failures came in steps? Before he married these foreign women, he must have thought long and hard about the issue. At least I hope he did. Wise diplomacy or obedience to Yahweh? Chances are he spoke with his advisers. Keep the peace or obey the Law? Perhaps some of the surrounding nations had armies that he, a scholar and inventor, did not want to deal with. In his mind he had more interesting and important things to do, one of which was building the Temple so that Israel could have a focal point from which to worship God. Yes, it was easier and safer to marry these foreign women of royal birth than to become a warrior like his father David. Solomon ruled for 40 years, and even assuming he was marrying before he assumed the throne, think of the number of weddings this man had! Maybe 15 to 20 a year!

After he made the decision to marry all these women, Solomon "held fast to them in love" and allowed them to keep their gods. Frankly, I don't understand how he even knew all of them, let alone loved them. Finally, he worshiped their gods, even Ashtoreth and the abominable Molech. How could such a wise man fall so low?

Solomon's commitment to God was undermined little by little by the "dailiness" and expedience of his life. Step by subtle step, he chose to act like a mighty king instead of a servant of the Most High God. Year by year, he compromised his standards until they no longer resembled God's. Slowly but inevitably, "his heart was not fully devoted to the LORD his God" and "he did not follow the LORD completely."

Granted, we don't normally make decisions on the scale of Solomon, but our choices will influence our lives and the lives of everyone we touch every bit as strongly as Solomon's decisions about his heathen wives and their gods impacted his.

We don't think about keeping a nation at peace, but we may think about lying to keep peace in the family. We don't have the spiritual lives of thousands upon thousands in our hands, but we directly or indirectly influence everyone we know toward Jesus or away from Him. We may not erect idols in the living room, but we can worship at the altar of stuff if we're not careful, and inevitably our children will too.

We must make our commitment to Christ firm, our fellowship with Him robust, our interactions with Him genuine. It's the only way to prevent being like Solomon. I know that when I die, I do *not* want people to speak of me as Scripture does of him, "His heart was not fully devoted to the LORD his God."

Rather, I want my life to have evidenced what Mark Buchanan calls "a living [faith], brim full of energy, feisty and sinewy and down to the bone." I want to be known as a servant of God, sufficient not in myself but in Him, following where He led, living as He wanted. I want to be like Paul who could write:

> I have fought the good fight, I have finished the race, I have kept the faith (*2 Tim. 4:7*).

Don't you?

God, we all want emotional consistency and control. The cost of achieving these things is everything and nothing— everything as we know of our lives, yet nothing compared to the benefits and blessings you will give us. May we in our commitment to you be a sweet fragrance, redolent with your love, to both you and to the world around us. Amen.

Summary

Commitment is rooting ourselves in Christ as our Anchor and our Provider.

Total commitment to God is at the core of emotional consistency.

The "dailiness" of life can undercut our commitment to God. Solomon is an example of this occurrence.

What Do You Think?

1. We have talked about digging our roots deep in Christ. Read Hebrews 12:15 and Deuteronomy 29:18. What do these verses warn about roots? _____

_____

_____

_____

2. The parable of the sower mentions the importance of roots. Read Matthew 13:21-22. What does it teach us about roots? _____

_____

_____

_____

3. When you think about committing your life to Christ completely, what gives you greatest concern or hesitation? ___

_____

_____

_____

4. Read Romans 14:8. How does the eternal perspective in this verse help you in thinking about commitment?

_____

_____

5. Read Philippians 3:7-10. How does Paul explain the depth of his commitment to Christ? _____

_____

_____

_____

How Do You Feel?

Rooted Commitment

Notes

Chapter 2

1. *Harvard Women's Health Watch* newsletter (June 2004), 4.

2. Edward T. Welch, *Counselor's Guide to the Brain and Its Disorders* (Grand Rapids: Zondervan Publishing, 1991), 30-31.

3. Ibid., 52.

4. Quoted in Gail Sheehy, "The Silent Passage of *Vanity Fair* (October 191).

Chapter 5

1. Oswald Chambers, *My Utmost for His Highest* (Westwood, N.J.: Barbour and Company, 1935, 1963), Aug. 9.

Chapter 6

1. Chambers, *My Utmost for His Highest,* Aug. 28.

2. Jerome and Kellie Daley, *Not Your Parents' Marriage* (Colorado Springs: Waterbrook Press, 2006), 22-23.

Chapter 10

1. Mark Buchanan, *Your God Is Too Safe* (Sisters, Oreg.: Multnomah Publishers, 2001).